At Fellowship of Christian Athletes, our core values are integrity, teamwork, excellence and serving. As athletes and people who care for others, Clayton and Ellen have risen to the challenge and live out these values. Their story shows they are champions whom young people can follow.

## Dan Britton
Senior Vice President of Fellowship of Christian Athletes

I believe that the more clearly we see God, the more joyfully we serve others for the sake of the gospel. Clayton and Ellen have clearly seen God in the person and work of Jesus, and they are joyfully serving others as a result. Clayton and Ellen's humility is evident in the way they treat others, the way they invest their time, and the way they serve. Clayton and Ellen have taken the teachings of Jesus to heart, and they're making a difference. Read their story and find out how you can as well.

## Brandon Cash
Pastor of Oceanside Christian Fellowship, El Segundo, California
Chaplain of the Los Angeles Dodgers

Clayton Kershaw has moved from good to great, both on and off the field. He and his wife, Ellen, have just scratched the surface of what they can become, and they challenge us to also reach much higher limits in our own lives.

## Orel Hershiser
1988 NL Cy Young Award Winner and World Champion Los Angeles Dodgers Pitcher

I have been inspired by the passion that Ellen and Clayton share for Zambia. The children and the bleak living conditions have left a lasting impression on them, and it is incredible to notice the Lord stirring in their hearts to make a difference. Partnering with the Kershaws is a joy. I've seen their love for Africa grow, and I thank God for the privilege of working together to impact the children that Arise Africa strives to help.

## Alissa Hollimon
President and Co-founder of Arise Africa

Sure, Clayton led the National League in wins last year and even won the pitching triple crown, and that's all great . . . but what's greater still are the thousands of life-changing wins he and his wife, Ellen, get to enjoy every day through their work with Arise Africa. We've got to grow more Clayton Kershaws—not just for the future of baseball, but also for the future of the world. God bless them!

## Frank Pastore
KKLA Radio Show Host, Author and Retired Major League Pitcher

# CLAYTON & ELLEN KERSHAW

WITH ANN HIGGINBOTTOM

# Arise

Live Out Your Faith and Dreams on Whatever Field You
Find Yourself *from the Major Leagues to Africa*

**Regal**

**From Gospel Light**
**Ventura, California, U.S.A.**

Published by Regal
From Gospel Light
Ventura, California, U.S.A.
*www.regalbooks.com*
Printed in the U.S.A.

All photos © 2011 the Kershaw family library, except photo #7, by Gail
and Laura Schultz; photos #21, #22, #23 and #26, by Juan Ocampo,
Los Angeles Dodgers; photo #25, by John SooHoo, Los Angeles Dodgers;
and photos #30 and #31 by Edmonson Photography.
Used with permission.

Library of Congress Cataloging-in-Publication Data
Kershaw, Clayton.
Arise : live out your faith and dreams on whatever field you find yourself /
Clayton Kershaw, Ellen Kershaw, with Ann Higginbottom.
p. cm.
ISBN 978-0-8307-6086-2 (hard cover)
1. Christian youth—Religious life. 2. Kershaw, Clayton. 3. Kershaw, Ellen. I. Kershaw,
Ellen. II. Higginbottom, Ann. III. Title.
BV4531.3.K48 2012
248.8'44—dc23
2011038408

Rights for publishing this book outside the U.S.A. or in non-English languages are
administered by Gospel Light Worldwide, an international not-for-profit ministry.
For additional information, please visit www.glww.org, email info@glww.org, or write
to Gospel Light Worldwide, 1957 Eastman Avenue, Ventura, CA 93003, U.S.A.

To order copies of this book and other Regal products in bulk quantities,
please contact us at 1-800-446-7735.

# DEDICATION

*Written with love and gratitude for our family and friends.*
*This is your story, too, and it wouldn't be the same without you.*
*We love you.*

*To Hope, and the children who share a story that is similar to hers.*
*You have inspired our lives more than you will ever know.*

*And to young readers who have big dreams that are worth chasing.*
*We are on that journey with you.*

# Contents

# Foreword

By A.J. Ellis, Catcher for the Los Angeles Dodgers

*As iron sharpens iron, so one man sharpens another.*

PROVERBS 27:17

The day after Clayton starts a game, long before the gates open and fans enter the stadium, he's already at work preparing for the next start. The fact that he's out there, ready to go the day, after isn't unique—most starting pitchers have a routine between starts. Weight lifting, conditioning and a throwing schedule are the norm. In fact, because most starters strictly follow this routine, they are considered stubborn, detailed and even superstitious. The ones who take it to the extreme are called crazy. Clayton is downright insane.

I know this firsthand, because I try to keep up with him the day after he starts. Meeting on the field, we run together, from foul pole to foul pole, at various intervals, lengths and speeds. We challenge and push each other, but honestly, I'm just trying to keep up with him. Because of who Kersh is, both on and off the field, he unintentionally sets the bar so high that my goal of simply keeping up is admirable. I know that if I can keep up with him, I'll improve—and more than just getting better at baseball.

I look forward to these post start runs because it's quiet time together. We share rare moments away from the clutter and commotion of the clubhouse and find space to talk about everything. We talk about the start he had the night before—how he felt, what pitches were working, the way he attacked certain hitters. We talk about the team and how we're playing, where we are in the standings, and things we can do to help secure a win. Finally, and most importantly, we talk about life. We remind each other of Scripture or talk about our weekly Bible study led by team chaplin Brandon Cash.

There are unique trials and temptations for Christians in professional baseball. With Kersh, I feel free to talk about the fears, doubts and struggles I'm facing. He does the same. We can talk about the strain baseball puts on family and how much our wives sacrifice for us to chase this game. I tell him about life as a baseball-playing father and the change that brings. He tells me about growing up in a single-parent home in Texas and the challenges that came with it. We offer advice and hold one another accountable. And when the run ends, we get ready for that night's game.

After the run is over, Clayton's insanity continues. He's not just passionate about being a great pitcher; he's passionate about being a great teammate, too. When he's not pitching, he's on the top step of the dugout supporting and cheering on the rest of us during the entire game. At a time when many players (especially starting pitchers) tend to disappear into the confines of the clubhouse or "food room," Clayton remains at his post.

His passion for winning and supporting the success of his teammates is genuine, and this is never more evident than on game day. After doing all he can to prepare between starts, Clayton walks into the clubhouse for his scheduled start with his "game face" on. For some pitchers this is a façade, simply to show their teammates that they are serious about the game. For Clayton, it is obvious to all of us that the fire inside is real and that this game is important. You can see and feel his drive and passion, and it makes us want to win for him. He lives out Colossians 3:23, "Whatever you do, work at it with all your heart, as working for the Lord, not for men."

In light of Clayton's passion to succeed on the field, you can imagine my shock when he told me last year that he and Ellen were going to spend the first two weeks of the new year in Africa on a missionary trip. I knew of Ellen's passion for missions and the impact it had on her life and spiritual growth, but I couldn't help but think, *Come on, really, Kersh?* Off-season is the peak training season for baseball players, and there would be no place for him to throw or work out in the middle of Africa. However, my perspective was quickly reversed when Clayton reminded me of something he had said before: "We should want to be known as Christians who happen to play baseball, not as baseball-playing Christians." Clayton is not just passionate; he's passionate for the right things.

Like Clayton, I encourage you to passionately embrace this challenge—the challenge of giving your all in every aspect of your life for the glory of God. Seek opportunities to reach out of your comfort zone to help those less fortunate overseas and even right across the street. Welcome a new perspective of being known first and foremost in this world as a Christian co-worker, a Christian spouse, a Christian parent or a Christian student. Embrace the words and wisdom of the Kershaws—a wise-beyond-their-years couple serving others for the kingdom of our Lord. In short, I invite you to do what I attempt to do when I run with Kersh and in every other part of my life—try and keep up!

# Introduction

What can anyone really accomplish in 23 years? If you listen to the world, you'd probably say, "Nothing significant." No one seems to expect young people to do much. If you try to be different, you hear that you're too naïve. If you have big dreams, you've lost touch with reality. There's no time for dreaming or making a difference. The rules of the game are clear: Pursue popularity, money and an identity in what you do. That's what society tells you, so you find yourself in a constant battle to believe that anything else matters.

We have heard all the same things you have, but we want to suggest an alternative. Youth brings a vibrant confidence—the courage to believe in unhindered possibilities. We think that is a beautiful thing. Many young people want to stand out, and they really can do great things. We are two young people who long to be different.

Lots of folks never figure this out, but life is not all about getting ahead. For whatever reason, we started challenging the norm years ago. We started asking big questions, and we found answers that made life more fulfilling and fun. Maybe you feel the pressure to play by the world's rules. We did—and we still do. We struggle, but our dreams and the desire to make an impact remain. Our hope is that you will ask, as we did, "What if my life looked different?"

To see life differently, one must find a new perspective. We are Christians, so that influences the way we tell our story. Everything changes when we see life through the lenses of our faith in Jesus Christ. We see that life is not about paychecks and status. Our greatest joy and meaning is found in our relationships with God and other people.

We have one of those crazy stories that you hear about every once a while. We started dating when we were 14 years old, when we were just awkward freshmen in high school. Eight years later, we got married. So our story covers a lot more than the first year of our marriage. A big part of our tale centers on growing up together.

From our perspective, we are on a journey of believing that God intends to use our lives for His glory.

This book shares our story. We hope that it will give you a window into our world of baseball, relationships and mission trips to Africa. But more than that, we hope that you will grow with us as we reflect on our experiences and our desire to live for something more than ourselves. If you are someone who professes faith in Christ, we want to encourage you to live out your faith exactly where you are. If you are someone who is still trying to figure out what you believe, know that we are still on the road, too. Perhaps something the Lord has taught us will be helpful to you. Maybe you picked up this book because you love baseball. So do we, and that's a big part of our story as well. We share in these pages a number of humorous and insightful stories about our journey in the Major Leagues. If you want to know more about what's going on in Africa, we are excited to share those experiences with you, too.

Whatever brings you here, we hope you'll come along with us. Our story takes us from the dirt of the pitching mound to the dirt roads of Zambia. Your story may be different in its details, but all of our stories unfold with incredible significance. You have a story to tell and a purpose to live out. We want a generation of young people to arise—to hope and believe that their lives are full of purpose. We want you to figure out your particular calling. We want you to know the joy that comes from giving more than you receive.

"The LORD has done great things for us, and we are filled with joy" (Ps. 126:3). He has been so gracious to us, and we long to respond by living for Him. Having received much grace, we hope to bring the Lord much glory. We have also found much joy along the way. Right where you are—God has a purpose for your life. We hope these stories of our journey will entertain and encourage you. Laugh with us. Enjoy baseball with us. Learn about Africa with us. Consider the rich plan God has for your life. Rise up to see it, and join us in striving to live for something more.

*Don't let anyone look down on you because you are young, but set an example for the believers in speech, in life, in love, in faith and in purity.*

1 TIMOTHY 4:12

# 1

# ONE IN A MILLION

Clayton

**Life is often defined by unexpected moments.** Sometimes we feel them coming, but more often than not, they sneak up on us. Other times, apparently small, insignificant moments are drawn together and collectively change our lives. You don't have to live 90 years to feel the weight of these particular moments. Your next moment could be a defining one. I am only 23 years old, but I can already identify certain moments that have had a lasting impact on me. These moments built courage, brought heartache, and taught me humility. They opened my eyes to my youthful pride and stubborn nature. I now see a little bit more clearly how God's grace was at work in a young kid who had a lot to learn and a determination to beat the odds. One moment in particular still stands out in my memory.

I was 14 years old—a gangly, slightly chubby freshman in high school. After a year of reveling in our reign as the big eighth-grade "men" on the middle school campus, my buddies and I were once again the smallest guys during passing period. We were back at the bottom of the totem pole. Everyone else seemed to have found the groove of high school. They were confident and smart—starters on the football, baseball and basketball teams. Upper classmen. We were humbled by a new school, new faces, and most of all, by the new pressure to find our voices among the multitudes. Sure, we knew we had work to do in the classroom. But my buddies and I were particularly interested in making a statement on the field.

In Texas, football takes precedence over just about every sport, even baseball. I was a big kid, so initially it seemed like a natural fit for me. Whatever I played, I just wanted to make an impact. Highland Park football has a great winning tradition, and it was a rush to be part of a team that was so established and legendary. We all felt the need to make a name for ourselves and prove to others that we were something. Playing football was a great way to begin high school—going out for the team, grinding through practices with friends, and representing our school during games created a strong sense of camaraderie and pride. Still, nothing captured my heart like baseball.

For the most part, I went into high school with all of my friends from middle school. There were some new faces on the first day of school, but more or less, my eighth-grade friends became my classmates at Highland Park High School. I had a tight-knit group of guys who had been my best friends since third grade. We did everything together, from sports to carpool to awkward eighth-grade dances. Before high school, we hadn't been too interested in girls, but slowly our group expanded, and we saw the social benefit of getting to know a few of them. In particular, there was one girl who caught my eye. Ellen was funny and seemed comfortable in her own skin. I enjoyed hanging out with her so much that I began going to great lengths just to be around her. That's how I found myself in an optional student leadership class that met for 13 weeks on Monday evenings. Not really my kind of thing . . . but Ellen was in it. The administration had recommended underclassmen who showed early signs of leadership. Ellen was a standout. I thought it would be fun to be in there with her.

The class met each Monday night for several hours. We discussed things like community involvement, service opportunities and leading by example as young high school students. I mastered the art of doodling on the back of my nameplate. One Monday, the topic turned to dreams and people of influence. That one class period—on that one ordinary Monday night—became a defining moment for me. The teacher went around the room and asked students to share about their dreams and the people who had been influential in their lives. My classmates gave plenty of well-reasoned responses, aspirations and a list of mentors that any teacher would love to hear. It was finally my turn, and fellow students swiveled in their chairs to hear what I would say. I knew my answer would probably get some critique from the teacher, but I was full of that youthful pride I mentioned earlier. I told everyone that the people of influence in my life were professional athletes. Then I confidently declared that my dream was to play baseball professionally.

There were a few chuckles from some friends in the back of the room who all knew where this was going. But I stood my ground, knowing somewhere in my heart that this was a dream worth stating, chasing and even defending. The teacher was gracious in his response, but he got right to the point. He explained to me that while goals were certainly important, we should always consider the odds. He reminded me of the statistics. High school athletes have a slim chance of playing college sports, and beyond that, college athletes have an even more depressingly slim chance of playing professionally. He didn't need to touch on the rarity of making it from the Minor Leagues to the Majors—I was well aware of that statistic as well. A hush fell over the room, and I could tell my classmates were a little uneasy. For a moment, I forgot that Ellen was nearby, listening to each word that came out of my mouth. With a hint of sarcasm, I told the teacher that he had crushed my dream. He quickly shifted gears and tried to encourage me. "I do want you to understand the odds, Clayton. They are one in a million. But the important thing is that you see yourself as the one. Don't think about the million. Visualize yourself being the one who makes it. You are the one. Be the one."

I smiled and nodded. I could have written his words off as a lame attempt to salvage my dream, but something actually clicked inside me at that moment. My teacher's comments inspired me to focus on the dream. He hit the nail on the head: Be the one. I started to visualize myself as the one who would make it. Through a teacher in an elective leadership class, the Lord lit a fire underneath me that propelled me toward becoming more of the man He intended me to be.

In one of his letters to his apprentice Timothy, the apostle Paul gives a powerful charge: "Don't let anyone look down on you because you are young, but set an example for the believers in speech, in life, in love, in faith and in purity" (1 Tim. 4:12). What Paul says to Timothy is exactly what I learned that evening in the Leadership 101 class. It doesn't matter how old you are—anyone can make an impact. Dreams are just dreams until you take a step toward them. Then the dream becomes a goal. Our culture today tells us that all of our goals and motivations should lead toward a better, more comfortable and more successful life for us. We don't have to listen long to get the message. The world tells us over and over, "Life is all about *you*." And yet I can't help but stop and ask, "What's it really all about?" Personal achievements matter, but only to a certain point. I decided in class that day not to allow the odds to define me. People could question my dream and my drive all day long, but in the end, the Lord had a plan for my life. I wanted the Lord to define me. I wanted my life to be all about Him.

As a freshman in high school, I was young and had a lot to learn. I still do. But even as a teenager sitting in a leadership class, I saw the opportunity to set an example. I knew that I loved baseball and that I wanted to play professionally. I also knew that the odds were tough, and people would do whatever it took to get there. If I could achieve this dream—and do so without compromising my principles or stepping on others to get ahead—surely God would be honored.

To this day, I still look back at that moment. I am grateful that it happened, and I am grateful for that teacher who spoke a bit of reality to a stubborn 14-year-old. More than anything, I am grateful to God for the dream He rooted deep in my heart. I set out at that young age to set an example for those who were watching. (Of course, I was hoping that Ellen would watch, too.) I was anxious to strive beyond personal achievement and dedicate my life to more than just getting ahead. It was a lofty dream of an overly confident kid in a freshman leadership class. But I am so thankful for that moment when I dared to believe that, by God's grace, I could be one in a million.

# 2

# WHEN YOUR PURPOSE
# GETS PUT ON HOLD

Ellen

**I am sitting in my old room at my parents' house.** I grew up in this house and lived here for 23 years before getting married. My room looks exactly the same today as it did when I was in high school. Sitting in my lap is my eighth-grade photo album. Back then, it was the cool thing to carry around a disposable camera and document every aspect of life. Now I'm sitting here wishing I hadn't followed that convention—or any of a number of others. Why did I think that "frosting" my dark brown hair was a good idea? Why did I think the bands on my braces needed to coordinate with the holiday of the month? Then there is the issue of fashion. My mom allowed me to step out of the house wearing velvet from head to toe—with an inch of midriff showing! Scrapbooks are life's way of keeping me humble.

Eighth grade is a funny phase of life. After years of feeling like a child, I was finally beginning to feel more grown up. The days of always being younger than someone in school were behind my classmates and me, and we were finally at the top of the pile. We were eighth-graders. For me, at age 13, boys were becoming friends and interests. Almost overnight, they went from gross and immature to mysterious and intriguing. High school was just a summer away, and my friends and I were all feeling confident that the next four years of our lives would be the best ever.

Still, there were humorous reminders that I had a lot of growing up to do. I was in the final stages of braces, desperately hoping that they would be gone by the time I made my high school debut. My legs seemed to grow faster than any other part of me—one of those funny disproportions that we don't really notice until we see a picture years later. Those pictures also revealed the ebb and flow of acceptable fashion. As if outfits archived in photographs aren't enough, my siblings won't let me forget my questionable, eclectic taste and favorite looks from the past. So what if leopard and zebra print never went out of style in my wardrobe?

Awkwardness aside, eighth grade was an important year in my life. For the first time, Africa became more than just a continent I had to know for geography class. Suddenly, it was a significant place on the map. That year, something started to stir in my heart that would forever change my life.

For my girlfriends and me, the after-school episodes of the *Oprah* show were part of the daily routine. I always made it home in time to settle in with a snack and watch legendary talk show host Oprah Winfrey. My friends and I would then gather in the halls before school the next day to discuss Oprah's breaking news. One afternoon's show caught my attention more than any other episode. Oprah was in Africa. She walked the streets, giving us glimpses into the extreme poverty that many Africans experience. She stopped and talked to people, asking them about their lives. Most intriguing to me, she knelt to hug children with beautiful, captivating faces.

My heart stood still as I watched her hour-long special unfold. I was drawn to the countries, the dire needs, and most of all to the people who filled the scenes. I realized more than ever that I was sheltered. I had grown up in a bubble where poverty didn't exist. I remember that day like it was yesterday. I stared at those precious children, and I was mesmerized—excited and terrified at the same time. Today I can recall very few things that Oprah said during the program, but I remember the faces. Something inside of me started to take shape at that moment. I was discovering a dream I never knew was in me. I'm amazed at how the Lord stopped me in my tracks, grabbed my heart, and turned it in a new direction. He planted in me a seed of desire to live for something bigger than myself. Something sparked that day—something that would change my life forever. A dream was born.

We all have dreams—every one of us. In His goodness, the Lord gives different and exciting dreams to each of us. Sometimes those dreams stay buried in our hearts for long seasons. But they are there, and it is a beautiful moment when they rise up and begin to bloom. Clayton's dream involved the dirt of a pitching mound. My dream carried me down the dirt roads of Africa. As eighth-graders, we never could have imagined that those two dreams would one day come true and collide. But the Lord had it planned out long ago. There is a dream inside of you. You might not be able to put it into words yet. Maybe it's buried too deep. I encourage you to dig for it. I can't wait for you to experience that "Aha!" moment when you finally figure it out.

I must have thought about that Oprah episode a million times in the years that followed. Somehow, deep in my gut, I knew that I would go to Africa one day. I would walk those dusty streets and hold those beautiful children with the captivating eyes. I had a feeling that they would change my life forever. In the meantime, I had to wait. I was only 14 years old. I was barely allowed to cross the street, let alone the Atlantic Ocean. If my siblings and I had a dream or a passion, our parents were enthusiastically supportive, but traveling to Africa alone was a little different from asking for another ballet class. I started dreaming about going to Africa that year, but for five years that dream was put on hold. I knew my parents were not ready to let me go, and somewhere in my heart, I knew that the Lord still had work to do in me as well. The dream was clear, however. God had sparked something in me, and that flame grew into a life purpose. When the time was right, I would see what it was all about.

Amazingly, when we have to put our purposes on hold, the Lord does not give up on us. In fact, He uses that time of waiting to prepare us for the next big thing. The Bible describes a season of waiting that took David from being a shepherd in the fields to being the king of Israel. David served the Lord as a shepherd, and that prepared him to be the shepherd of God's people. All the long, dark nights of counting sheep and warding off dangers were not wasted. They were extremely significant. During those years, the Lord took an ordinary boy with an ordinary profession and did something extraordinary in him. While tending sheep, David came to know the Lord as his personal Shepherd. Through that relationship, he began to understand how to shepherd God's people.

David's time of waiting and listening to God inspired him to write a familiar psalm, describing God's love for him:

> The LORD is my shepherd, I shall not be in want.
> He makes me lie down in green pastures,
> he leads me beside quiet waters,
> he restores my soul.
> He guides me in paths of righteousness for his name's sake.
> Even though I walk through the valley of the shadow of death,
> I will fear no evil, for you are with me;
> your rod and your staff, they comfort me.
> You prepare a table before me in the presence of my enemies.
> You anoint my head with oil; my cup overflows.
> Surely goodness and love will follow me all the days of my life,
> and I will dwell in the house of the LORD forever (Ps. 23).

The Lord had something great planned for David's life, and David's years as a shepherd were crucial in preparing him for that plan. When I was 14, the Lord planted a seed in my heart that would take years to bloom. When your purpose gets put on hold, God has a great and beautiful reason. Even the time of waiting has great intention because the Lord is graciously in control. In the summer of 2007, I made my first trip across the ocean by myself. I am certain that I would not have been ready without those five years of waiting.

Sometimes we expect these opportunities to hit us between the eyes or to be handed to us on a silver platter. We hope that they will present themselves as offers that we just can't turn down. For me, I kept waiting for the "perfect" chance to go . . . like finding a friend to be adventurous with me and decide we were both called to Zambia. But I knew this nagging passion wasn't going anywhere anytime soon. I had to take initiative and figure it out on my own. I had to chase it.

My dear friend Charlotte had been to Zambia before, and I knew it had changed her life. The thought of putting off a life calling for one more summer was burdensome. Charlotte gave me the loving push that I needed. She calmed my fears about the plane flight and what I would eat once I got there. We talked about what it would be like to leave Africa once I had fallen in love with the children. I had to face the reality of going alone—something that was overwhelming to me. I came to terms with the fact that this was going to be a "table for one" experience, but I found peace in knowing that the Lord had brought me this far. He wasn't going to make me face it alone. The Lord had burned those precious faces from the television on my heart, and then finally, I was there. The people of Africa were no longer a nameless statistic or two-dimensional images on a screen to me. Now I knew specific faces and names and stories.

King David served God's purpose in his own generation (see Acts 13:36). Lord willing, I long to do the same. As a long-legged adolescent, I discovered a dream. There is something incredibly freeing about receiving a God-sized dream from the Lord. For five years, I waited for that purpose to unfold—and when I stepped off the plane in Zambia years later, I knew it was worth the wait. Somehow a place I had only seen on television seemed strangely familiar. For the first time in my life, I took a deep breath of Zambian air and planted my feet on African soil. I was finally home.

# 3

# WHO AM I?

Clayton

**True story:** One of the first baseball teams I ever played for was the Dodgers. Nothing could beat sporting that Dodger blue for the first time. After our games, we would chow down on fruit snacks and soft drinks in our carpool. My friends and I would blast "Eye of the Tiger" and hang our heads out of every window. My first experience as a Dodger was epic.

Growing up, Little League Baseball was life for me. I loved playing all sports, but nothing was more exciting than playing baseball with my best friends. We were assigned to various teams with Major League names, matching hats and uniforms. It was fun to suit up like guys in the big leagues. We each picked the number of our favorite baseball player. Mine was always #22, for the crazy-good lefthander Will Clark, first baseman for the Texas Rangers at the time. For my buddies and me, it was cool just to be part of a team and wearing the uniforms. As I got older, I joined different teams for school, fall ball, spring ball and summer league. With each new season, I received a new uniform and a new set of guys to identify with. Teammates, colors and cleat sizes changed each season. The ball got harder to hit as the pitches flew faster to the plate. Nothing stayed the same—except my intense desire to play ball.

I would wear my team hat for a season and then toss it in a pile of sweat-stained baseball caps and beat-up cleats. My mom tried to keep up with the parade of trophies that lined my bookshelves. Each season, the old ones got shoved to the back to make room for the new ones, but they were all worthy of display. I was the only guy I knew with a patchwork ceiling of team jerseys stapled into place. The trophies and jerseys were all dusty reminders of good times with friends, improving skills, and a growing desire to get better. I don't think I realized it then, but those small trophies were more than prizes. Each of those gilded plastic awards could ignite a memory of a significant strikeout, a double play, a bus ride home, a teammate's homerun that earned the win, or victory cannonballs in the pool afterwards. These statues not only represented my love for the sport, but they also served as reminders of the identity I took on with each new team.

Fast-forward to today. Those old sweaty hats are now safely stowed in a box next to an army of jumbled trophies. They meant something to me in the past, because I felt like they were symbols of who I was as a baseball player. Cardinal crimson, Dodger blue, Mustang red, Highland Park navy and gold—I knew who I was by the jersey I wore and the guys who played with me. I can almost see the passing of time—with each jump from one team to the next, new faces and moments played their role in shaping the identity of a kid inspired by a game but looking to find himself in so much more.

Life is filled with the constant question: "Who am I?" We spend so much of our time attempting to answer that question, whether we realize it or not. Starting at a young age, we all try to figure out who we are. We are looking for something to grab onto.

Figuring out who we are is really the work of a lifetime. It is valid to identify with school, friends, family or even a team. But without Christ at the core, there is not a central focus. I came to know more about the Lord in high school through a SportsPlus Bible study led by a guy named Steve Kirwan. This study gave my buddies and me a chance to dig below the surface with one another, hearing personal prayer requests and figuring out what it meant to have a consistent identity in Christ. I had to learn how to fight to find my identity in the Lord. That battle continues to this day. Change seems to be a constant in life and in Major League Baseball. As I move between teams, cities and teammates, my identity in Christ is the only true consistency that matters. Change happens, so it's a good practice to get used to it. Uncertainties like switching schools or teams can bring out anxiety in the most level-headed person. We all have different stories, but I am certain that in some way, fitting in is a common theme for us all. The key is figuring out who we are in Christ.

The truth is, things change, people grow up, and graduation can scatter your friends across the country. Sometimes a new beginning can feel like square one, and we are back to figuring out who we want to be in the next phase of life. I remember having that feeling when I came into the Minor Leagues. No one cared who I was, apart from the fact that I was a lefthander from Texas, trying to climb the ladder of the Minors to get to the Majors like everyone else. It occurred to me that people wouldn't know I was a Christian unless the Lord was evident in my life. (Just like they wouldn't know that I could tear it up at Ping-Pong unless I challenged someone to a duel.) On the outside, I looked exactly like everyone else: a baseball player.

The Lord did something remarkable in my life as I wrestled with the old question—"Who am I?" I remember realizing in high school that life changes a lot, and so we have to root ourselves in something that is much bigger and more consistent than ourselves, our friends or our individual identities. In the Gospel of Matthew, Jesus asks the disciples to answer a question. However, Jesus really refines the question, making His own identity more important than any other identity:

> "But what about you?" he asked. "Who do you say I am?"
> Simon Peter answered, "You are the Christ, the Son of the living God" (Matt. 16:15-16).

Jesus asks the disciples who He is, not who they are. Knowing who you are in relationship to God will transform the way you see yourself and your identity. The more I understand who God says He is, the more I understand who I am. Because God is my Father, I am His child. Because of Christ, I have salvation. Because of who He is, I know that my identity is secure . . . in Him. Everything else can change, but Jesus Christ is the same yesterday, today and forever (see Heb. 13:8).

It is good to know that the Lord gives us a lifetime to work out our identities and sort out who we are in Christ. His calling for our lives will undoubtedly compete with daily struggles of temptation to take an easier path. The battle to maintain a Christ-centered identity is the most worthy fight we will face.

There are other identities that demand our attention every day. I am a son, a friend, a husband and a baseball player. There are times in my life when one focus overshadows the other, and that's when I realize how easy it is to lose sight of who I am. These other identities are significant, but they are not ultimate. When I make them ultimate, I am asking them to bear a weight they were never designed to hold. Family, friends and careers can be consistent blessings in our lives, but they cannot bear the weight of defining us. When Christ is ultimate, other people and other things are given freedom to play the roles in my life that the Lord intended them to play.

Having an identity in Christ brings great peace and simplicity. I can throw a miserable game or read a negative review and walk away, knowing that what people think about me is not everything. Failures and criticism are just small reminders that I am a work in progress. Identity in Christ gives freedom to my days, games and relationships.

Challenge yourself every morning. Ask, "Who am I?" and be honest about it. Whether you realize it or not, every day you'll answer that question one way or another. If you let that daily question lead you to Jesus, you will find the only absolutely secure place to find your identity. When you know who you are in Christ, you'll be amazed at the freedom and joy that fill your life.

# WHEN IT'S TIME TO GO

Ellen

June 2, 2007

*Dear Clayton,*

*Holy cow—I am getting on a plane to go to Africa tomorrow! I'm sitting in my room here in Dallas. My malaria pills are packed, and toilet paper rolls are stuffed in every crevice of my suitcase. (You really don't want to run out of that in Africa.) I also have enough People magazines to last me 22 hours on a plane. I'm nervous, but so excited at the same time. As you know, going to Africa has always been my dream. We have always talked about our dreams—your dreams, my dreams, our friends and their dreams. Do you remember when we were eighth-graders, and in the midst of my obsession with Oprah, my life was changed while watching her special on Africa? Since that day, I have dreamed about meeting those precious kids and finally being brave enough to go over there. I can't believe that tomorrow is the day. Can you believe it?*

*I feel so blessed that God gave me this passion, because it seems unique. My heart literally aches with anticipation—this is what I've been called to do. It's like I can't deny it anymore. My prayer journals are filled with prayers, asking for the opportunity to someday figure out this strong desire. I've longed to finally feel brave enough to take this leap of faith. I have come up with excuse after excuse. It is as if there was a quiet knock on my door for years . . . and tomorrow, I'm finally going to answer it! All of the pieces are fitting together for this summer, starting in the morning. Any suggestions on ice-breaking games to play with strangers I sit next to on the plane?*

*Right now, you are in the throes of another Minor League summer in Midland, Michigan. I am so proud of the way you have jumped into it again this year. I know this is your dream come true.*

*Being home with you over the off-season was awesome, but I am continually reminded that we are both right where we need to be. You need to be playing baseball. It seems that I need to go to Africa. Someday, I hope that you can come with me. But for now, I'm excited to go on this God-centered adventure on my own. It's scary going by myself, but I'm thinking that it's this way for a reason. Maybe I need to learn to be fully reliant on the Lord. Thank you for believing in this dream with me. Thanks for being my prayer warrior while I'm over there. I cannot wait to tell you all about the Lord's great work halfway across the world. And if I fall in love with a child over there . . . well, just don't be surprised if I bring one home.*

*Love, Ellen*

I sent that email the night before I flew to Africa for the first time. Clayton was beginning his second summer playing baseball in the Minor Leagues, this time in Midland, Michigan. I was about to embark on a journey that I had been dreaming of since I was 14 years old. After years of convincing my parents that I was equipped to handle the responsibility of international travel—and to Africa of all places—it was time to go.

We arrived at the airport with plenty of time remaining to let the enormity of the occasion sink in. This was it. I had dreamed of and waited for this day. I was anxious. However, the moments of anxiety were overwhelmed by the consistent sense that I was right where the Lord had called me to be. There is no greater peace than when you are right in the middle of God's sovereign will for your life.

I had just finished my freshman year of college. Clayton and I had made it successfully through our first year of long-distance dating. In between classes and sorority parties, I had jumped on planes to visit Clayton at Minor League ballparks around the country. Our worlds were very different, but that just gave us more to talk about and more to catch up on. He had new friends, and so did I. I listened to his dream of making it past the Minors to the Majors. He listened to my dream of facing my fears and someday going to Africa.

Throughout that year, the thought of not going to Africa had given me more anxiety than the idea of actually going had. I knew that I would be turning away from my calling if I were to ignore that desire. I had never been on a mission trip or out of the country. I had never really been anywhere by myself! I didn't know a single person on the flight with me, and yet I somehow hugged my mom and dad goodbye. Peace flowed through me. I was finally doing what I knew I should be doing. After five years of waiting, the time had come for me to go.

I signed up to go with a missions organization that had a ministry based in Lusaka, Zambia. My heart was to build relationships with the people of Zambia—I didn't just want to share my faith and move on; I wanted to spend hours with the same children every day. I was prepared to meet children with tough stories and do my best to show them Christ's love. The mission included spending an entire week with the same group of 10 Zambian orphans. Even if it was only for a week, I longed for them to experience unconditional love and the joy of being a child.

I clutched my brand-new passport in my hand. The thought of a stamp from Zambian customs christening my book thrilled me. I waved to my parents until they were out of sight. The plane was filled with people from around the world: some traveling on business, some returning home, all of them strangers to me. I was on the way to Africa, via London. Nothing could have been more exciting. I found my seat and quickly tucked away my backpack after slipping out my Bible, journal and a pen. I wrote, "Day One: Going to Africa" at the top of the page and then sat there, contemplating the vastness of that simple statement. I was going to Africa. By myself. I was answering a calling that had been weighing on my heart for five years. Thumbing through my Bible, I ran across a familiar passage that had encouraged and convicted me that past year:

> In the year that King Uzziah died, I saw the Lord seated on a throne, high and exalted, and the train of his robe filled the temple. Above him were seraphs, each with six wings: With two wings they covered their faces, with two they covered their feet, and with two they were flying. And they were calling to one another:

"Holy, holy, holy is the Lord Almighty; the whole earth is full of his glory."

At the sound of their voices the doorposts and thresholds shook and the temple was filled with smoke.
"Woe to me!" I cried. "I am ruined! For I am a man of unclean lips, and I live among a people of unclean lips, and my eyes have seen the King, the LORD Almighty."
Then one of the seraphs flew to me with a live coal in his hand, which he had taken with tongs from the altar. With it he touched my mouth and said, "See, this has touched your lips; your guilt is taken away and your sin atoned for."
Then I heard the voice of the Lord saying, "Whom shall I send? And who will go for us?"
And I said, "Here am I. Send me!" (Isa. 6:1-8).

I found myself in Isaiah's shoes. I understood in new ways the awestruck wonder that must have filled him. The Lord Almighty, in His thunderous power, was calling him to go and to serve. I thought about the fear that must have filled Isaiah as he considered such a daunting task—and yet what grabbed my attention was his faithful, confident reply: "Here am I! Send me!" I wrote those two short sentences over and over again in my journal as the plane prepared to depart.

When it's time to go, your heart feels like it might explode if you don't take a step forward. The Lord's perfect timing had me wait five years from my first thought of Africa to the day I stepped foot in Zambia. I don't know if I could have waited one more day. I longed to see something more and to be a part of something bigger than myself. I was also excited to get out of my day-to-day life in Texas. Things had become so routine for me there. Even college, the newest chapter of my life, had become comfortable. I knew that going to Zambia would be anything but comfortable. It was totally uncharacteristic of me—but I could hardly wait to take this leap of faith. It was a world I had only dreamed about and yet a place that seemed to be written into the fabric of my heart. I knew that I was exactly where I was supposed to be.

As the plane pulled away from the terminal, I sat with my nose pressed against the window. It was humbling to believe that this was actually going to happen. I looked down at the journal in my lap. "Here am I! Send me!" Sometimes a leap of faith seems more like a jump over the Grand Canyon. That's exactly how I felt on that first flight to Africa. The hours over the Atlantic gave me plenty of time to work through the fear and apprehension of the unknown and to remember the excitement of the journey ahead. When you move toward the Lord's will, there is a good chance you will find those two competing emotions: fear and excitement. I cannot imagine where I would be today if I had let fear win in my heart. I would have missed Africa!

Perhaps there is an area in your life where the Lord is calling you to step out in faith. It may seem unknown and risky, but I hope that you will take it. The Lord's plan for your life is beautiful and life-giving. Sometimes it requires grand leaps of faith—or in my case, swan dives over the Atlantic Ocean. When it's time to go, I hope that you will go forward by faith. Just as my leap toward Africa changed my life, taking your own step of faith may well transform yours.

# 5

# OUR GOD IS THE GREAT KING

Clayton

**As a kid, I spent most of my time outside.** No matter the season, there was always an activity. Snow is a rare sight in Dallas during the winter, but whenever we got some, my friends and I had a great time throwing balls of slush and ice at each other. "Pool hopping" became an annual summer activity for us. We would hop any fence that we knew had a pool on the other side of it and cannonball in, one after the other. Fall was football season. And spring was baseball season. Those were my four seasons—that simple and that great. The more time I spent outside during these seasons of my life, the more I became aware of the world around me—and how creation changed over the course of the year.

I remember thinking about how incredible the world is. I would consider the people, the places, the mountains, the trees and the beaches that fill the earth. It was overwhelming to me to think about how all of these things came to be. I had difficulty believing that all of the beauty in front of me had just evolved. Romans 1:20 says, "For since the creation of the world God's invisible qualities—his eternal power and divine nature—have been clearly seen, being understood from what has been made, so that men are without excuse." God's divine nature can be seen in everything. Creation pointed me to the Creator. As I built a slushy snowman, cooked an egg on the hot sidewalk, raked leaves into a front-yard fort, or took the pitcher's mound for another opening day of baseball season, I would think, *There's got to be something more to all of this. There's got to be Someone out there who makes the seasons change as they do.*

My first thoughts about "something more" and about God came from thinking about creation. It blew me away to look at the world around me—how could it have just come into being? That didn't make any sense to me. I knew I wasn't here by chance.

I knew the world was no accident. The Lord grabbed hold of my heart by showing Himself to me in all that He had made.

I grew up going to church every Sunday. Starting at a young age, I became familiar with God's Word through Sunday School lessons. I was never fully invested in my faith, though—it was just something that I grew up with. It was a collection of different things that people had told me about God. Gradually, however, I came to see that my faith wasn't just something to have in the back of my mind. I came to realize that this God I had been learning about was a Person who knew me and had a plan for me. I wanted to know more about that plan—and the Person behind it.

When I realized that I could have a personal relationship with God, I began by relating to Him as a great King. I was blown away by His creation and goodness in the world. It seemed fitting that I should worship Him with great reverence. Psalm 95:3 painted the picture of my God: "For the LORD is the great God, the great King above all gods." God was bigger, more majestic and more powerful than anyone or anything else I could imagine. As I grew in my faith, my prayers and thoughts were filled with awe and admiration for my King.

This vision of a great King led me to understand some really amazing things about the Lord. I learned that He is all-powerful and completely in control of our lives. Even for a kid growing up with a comfortable life in Dallas, knowing that God was in control of my life meant something to me. His grace was amazing to me. I could choose to walk with the Lord, or I could choose to go my own way. But God had given me a hunger to know Him. That seemed pretty generous to me. Until high school, I kept God at a safe distance. I knew that I wanted Him in my life, but I also thought that He could squash me like a bug. I had tremendous respect for God, but I focused almost exclusively on Him as King. As a result, I was missing so much about His character.

When I entered high school, the Lord brought friends and mentors into my life who helped shape my faith. For example, as I got to know Ellen, I noticed that she viewed God differently than I did. God was her friend, and she could talk to Him throughout the day. That side of God was new to me. I came to realize that if I only saw God as a King, I would miss the reality that He is a faithful friend and a loving Father. The thought of God as a heavenly Father was revolutionary to me. How could Someone so great love me that much? For the first time, I recognized the imbalance in my life. I was only seeing part of the picture. God is a great King. But He is also so much more than that. He is a Father who loves me and cares about having a personal relationship with me. I see this in the way He sent His Son to come after me. He refused to let me stay the same.

If you had a recording of my prayers today, you would probably conclude that I still view God as a great King. His power and might still do amaze me. But I hope you would also hear me learning to approach God as my Father. His grace and love toward me continue to change me. I still feel more comfortable praising God and worshiping His might than I do talking to Him casually as a Friend. However, I am growing in my understanding that God is so much more than any one thing. I want to enjoy all that He is. When we focus on just one aspect of the Lord, we shrink Him down and put Him in a box. But a real vision of God keeps us amazed, because we can't wrap our minds around how big He is. How can He be all of this at the same time?!

If you're like I am, you're probably tempted to relate to God in one particular way. Whatever aspect of His character you focus on, remember that the Lord is that and so much more. I grew up hearing about God. Maybe that's not your story. That's okay. You don't have to grow up in a Christian family or in church to start walking with the Lord today. It's not too late to start. When I look back at my life, I am grateful that the Lord captured my heart at a young age. However, I am even more thankful for how much He has taught me in recent years. Your personal relationship with God really does matter. Knowing Christ has made a world of difference in my life—through high school and now in baseball.

As a kid, I knew that there had to be something beyond and behind the creation and seasons that I saw. God led me to ask some big questions that He used to draw me closer to Him. Since then,

I have learned so much about God not only as a great King, but also as a Father and a Friend. The more I get to know Him, the more I realize how glorious He is. I don't think we'll ever arrive at a full understanding of who God is. How could we grasp the fullness of a God who is infinite? What an incredible thought! Every day we have an opportunity to grow in our knowledge of the Lord. The more we know Him, the more we enjoy Him—and, amazingly, the more we become like Him.

# Our God
# Is a Great Friend

Ellen

**I had 20 of my best friends in my wedding party on December 4, 2010.** It didn't make sense to keep it small. Those 20 girls really are my dearest friends and truly the most loyal people in the world. The idea of having so many best friends may sound funny, but to me it makes perfect sense. On my wedding day, I wanted to be surrounded by the girls who know my heart before the Lord—trusted friends I can count on to ask good questions about my walk with God, and about my relationship with Clayton. When it came down to it, 20 girls fit that description perfectly. My older sister, Ann, was my matron of honor. She knows me better than anyone. We shared a room for the first half of my life. Late night talks in bed with Ann led me into a deeper relationship with the Lord. I was deeply honored to have Ann and the rest of these amazing women surrounding me on my wedding day.

Ever since I was little, my life revolved around weekend plans with friends. For years, the big question seemed to be: "Who will go with me to the football game this Friday night?" I considered myself a pretty outgoing person, like the rest of my friends. We all had social agendas that we thought our lives depended on. As the third of four kids, I grew up amid the chaos of siblings and cousins. Our community was filled with generations of families and lots of activities for every age. Twice a year, we closed our street to cars and held block parties. We skated or biked down the middle of the street until it got dark. I loved walking to elementary school with the neighborhood kids. Ann would pull me (and our backpacks) in a red wagon. Being part of a community of people was second nature to me.

By the time I reached middle school, nothing mattered more to me than being included in a good group of friends. We had recently discovered the whole phenomenon of chatting online, which made it easier to talk to boys with confidence. Think about it: You can type, retype, seek advice from a friend, and then send a cool, witty response to a boy. It was the perfect way to communicate, but it also had so many hidden downsides. Girls would say confrontational things online that they would never have the guts to say in person. Relationships took their first steps in a chat room: "Will you go out with me?" It was as simple as that. Guys totally got off the hook if a girl said no. Feelings were hurt, conversations could be copied and shared, and things could be easily misinterpreted. Drama was just beginning.

Doesn't everybody have one school year that they remember as "the worst ever"? Mine was probably eighth grade. For the first time, I recognized that being included by friends mattered more to me than most other things. It made me miserable. I hadn't realized that I was being sucked into conditional friendships. A girl could be your best friend one day and your biggest nightmare the next. We all walked on eggshells around one another, trying to please everyone and stay in the middle of every conversation. We did whatever it took not to be the one left out. Though we never talked about it, there was a constant unspoken fear that friendships were in danger of being compromised or betrayed. Like most girls in eighth grade, I tried to find a secure spot in a group.

It took my own personal journey through torturous middle school drama to finally understand that no one was safe from a broken heart. Including myself, girls didn't always realize how hurtful their words and actions could be. At the time, I had no idea how much it would have meant to reach out to someone who didn't quite fit in. I wish I had known in middle school what I know today: People matter. As I went through that difficult year, I began to see something about the Lord that was refreshing to me. I read about His compassion toward people: "The LORD is compassionate and gracious, slow to anger, abounding in love" (Ps. 103:8). Abounding in love and compassionate. Those characteristics caught my attention because they were so different from what I saw all around me.

The story of the prodigal son is a picture of the Lord's compassion for us. He holds no record of wrong and loves the unlovable. The truths in that parable came to life for me. Luke 15 describes a lost son returning home to his father after a season of squandering his inheritance in reckless living. The father greets his wayward son with such incredible compassion. He clothes his son in his finest robe and throws a banquet of celebration. There is no mention of wrongs committed or the unworthiness of the son's behavior. There is only overflowing compassion for a son who once was lost but now is found. The son does not deserve the father's love. He could not meet the conditions of that love. Rather than punish his son, the father absorbs his son's guilt and shame so that his son can receive the gift of his love. That's exactly what Jesus did for us in dying for our sins.

I grew up knowing about the Lord's love for me. My parents showed me His love every day, and my Sunday School teachers reminded me of it every week. But unconditional love didn't mean a whole lot to me until I was desperate for it. When my social life was shaken in middle school, God graciously drew me to Himself. Clayton talks with reverence about God being a great King. For me, coming to know the Lord as my great Friend rescued me in eighth grade, and I found incredible joy in Him. I fell back on the faith I had known since I was little. The end of middle school was the beginning of figuring out my personal faith. I began to look to the Lord when things didn't make sense, and I found great comfort in Him.

The Lord was the faithful Friend I had struggled to find in other people. In Christ, I found a Friend whose love was always abundant. I poured myself into learning more about my faith and praying for His steadfast guidance to strengthen my walk with Him. There's not a cookie-cutter formula for doing that, so I turned to the discipline that came most naturally to me—prayer. Praying was easy for me because it was like talking to a friend. I would pray out loud, and I often wrote my prayers down in a journal. Confiding in the Lord with questions and uncertainties, I found comfort in the thought that He knew the depths of my heart and still loved the imperfect me. I am thankful to still be growing in my relationship with the One who knows me so well.

Over the years, I've thought more about the connection between desire and discipline. I didn't understand why prayer came so naturally to me and other things didn't. I struggled to spend meaningful time reading and studying God's Word. Discipline involves submitting to a process and doing something because we know we need it. I know that I need God's Word in my life. I know that I need to spend time with the Lord, but my desires often waver. I am learning, however, that I can pray for the Lord to give me a fresh desire even as I discipline myself to do what I know He is calling me to do. As I have practiced the spiritual disciplines, the Lord has been faithful to give me a growing desire for Him and His Word.

Knowing God as a great Friend has changed me. It affects the way I understand and worship Him. It has also changed the way I see people. Being a friend to others really is significant, because our friendships give us opportunities to show the love of Jesus to others. The girls I lived with in college became like family to me. They saw me at my best, they saw me at my worst, and they loved me through it all. We taught each other how to do laundry. More importantly, we taught each other that fabric softener is not the same thing as detergent. We taught each other to cook without sending the house up in flames. We traded clothes and often piled into one bed to stay up all night talking. We played pranks on each other and threw surprise costume parties. We had family dinners on Sunday evenings and encouraged one another toward dreams and goals. I was able to experience Christian community. What a precious gift from the Lord to see what loyal love looks like! We became a household of best friends who cared deeply for one another. It was only natural for me to ask these girls to stand with me on my wedding day.

I believe that some of God's greatest gifts in life come in the form of Christ-centered friends. My prayer is that you will experience friendships that build you up as a person. I hope you have friends who will share your joys and hold you accountable, even when it feels uncomfortable. I pray that you know God's love through meaningful friendships. During my four years at Texas A&M University, I found my kindred spirits—girls who helped me become the person the Lord wanted me to be.

Friendships matter. But more than any other, the friendship I have with the Lord changes things. When our identity is set in the Lord, things and people find their proper places in our lives. As we grow in our friendship with Him, we begin to care about people more than ever before. In the Gospel of John, Jesus talks about what it looks like to love people:

> My command is this: Love each other as I have loved you. Greater love has no one than this, that he lay down his life for his friends. You are my friends if you do what I command. I no longer call you servants, because a servant does not know his master's business. Instead, I have called you friends, for everything that I learned from my Father I have made known to you (John 15:12-15).

Jesus' desire to be my friend led Him to a cross. The greatest love the world has ever seen was on display as Jesus laid down His life for His friends. I will never be able to be the kind of friend I want to be unless I understand what Jesus has done for me. The more I know His love, the more I want that love to flow through me to all the people who need it. If you don't already, I hope that you will come to see God as a great Friend. It will change the way you love people. Most incredible of all, it will change you.

# 7

# GROWING UP TOGETHER

## Clayton

**It is pretty rare to marry the girl you asked out between classes during freshman year of high school. But that is exactly my story.** I was 14 years old, average height and slightly chubby. Ellen and I had run in the same circles for a few years, starting in middle school, so my friends were her friends. She stood out from the other girls because she seemed to take notice of people. She was also funny . . . for a girl. That was particularly interesting to me. She liked to laugh, and she even found some of my lame jokes funny. I knew that was too good to be true.

I officially asked Ellen to be my girlfriend in the hallways of Highland Park High School. We were racing between classes, but I thought the timing was perfect. I could ask her out and then take off, leaving little time for awkward small talk. She was cool about it and graciously accepted my invitation to be something more than friends. Relieved, I headed over to the cafeteria, where I was greeted with fist pumps and high fives by my friends. I had a girlfriend. We talked on AOL at night and never spent a single moment alone together. But we were "going out." Classic. I didn't realize it then, but that day changed my life. It marked the beginning of something that would unfold in ways I couldn't have imagined. Eight years later, I stood at the end of a church aisle and watched Ellen come through the doors and walk toward me. People say that kind of thing doesn't happen. Though I know we are an exception, our story proves that theory wrong.

Ellen and I grew up together. Though our relationship wore the "dating" tag, she was just like a best friend to me—someone with whom I could be completely myself. She was the first person I really opened up to. Together, we walked through awkward times and memorable times. It's funny that our dating relationship can be summed up in pictures from homecoming dances, proms and parties. We were quite a sight to behold at that first homecoming dance. I wore moccasins and a suit with a pink shirt. I had lost my last baby tooth right before the dance, so I had a hole in the front of my smile. Ellen had recently decided to "frost" her hair—whatever that means. That was a rough year for both of us.

I don't have any brothers or sisters, but Ellen's family quickly became mine. Her siblings treated me like I was one of them. The first summer after we started dating, I was invited to go on their annual family vacation to the beach. I'm not sure why we thought this was a good idea—Ellen and I had never spent a moment together without our group of friends around—but I went. For the first time, I was surrounded by the chaos of cousins, aunts, uncles and siblings. It was overwhelming that first year, but I loved every moment of it. We took pictures on the beach, and for the first time, I was thrown into the shot. Whether I was ready for it or not, her family pulled me right in. So much of our growing up together included our families. We joined forces for holidays and family dinners. The Melsons and the Kershaws blended together in a way that made us feel like more than a dating couple. It felt like family.

As a result, our relationship in high school didn't look like many others. We really didn't want it to. From the beginning, we talked about looking and acting different. When a guy and a girl date in high school, there's definitely potential for awkwardness for the people around them. We made it our goal never to be a couple that people felt uncomfortable being around. We hated the thought of someone feeling like a "third wheel." We wanted people to feel significant and welcome around us. Making people feel important was something that I saw Ellen do naturally. I wanted to be the same way. So in our relationship, we really tried to make others feel important. This started with our friends and family. But as the years went by, we also saw it play out in our new worlds. Ellen taught me a lot about loving others. When I'm on the baseball field for practice or in the clubhouse with the guys, I have a responsibility to make my teammates more important than myself. I learned in high school with Ellen that people respond when you show a genuine interest in them.

The first time I went to Africa with Ellen, I watched the way she loved the people. When you make someone feel appreciated and loved, walls come down and opportunities arise. I remember holding a young Zambian orphan named Jenny. She wrapped her arms around my neck, and we just sat there for a long time. It didn't take much to make Jenny feel significant—that someone would hold her was enough. What I saw in Africa was really no different from what I see in America. God does amazing work when we realize that people matter. Our time doing ministry in Africa was really about loving the people and praying that the Lord would use that to make a difference in their lives. The children that I met with Ellen had been told their entire lives that they were insignificant and worthless. But Christ changes things. How I respond to people really does matter. I'm thankful for the lesson that I started learning as a freshman in high school. Ellen and I wanted to have an outward focus. We didn't want to be unapproachable or awkward. We wanted to be together with our friends. Making that a priority made all the difference in our relationship.

Part of growing up together involved figuring out our faith. By God's grace, Ellen and I both grew up going to church and hearing about the Lord. By the time we reached high school, we had both plugged into our local Fellowship of Christian Athletes huddle sessions. It was cool to see our friends step up to lead worship songs and pray in front of hundreds of our peers. Being surrounded by Christian friends throughout high school was a huge blessing to us. We found accountability in our walks with Christ, and still had a lot of fun together on the weekends. As we grew in the Lord, we learned so much about identity. Any relationship carries the risk of making the other person an idol. It would have been really easy to make my friends and Ellen everything in my world. They were such a huge part of it. But the Lord started showing me early on that no one else could be my identity. The temptation in high school is to find your identity in your boyfriend or girlfriend, or in your group of friends. Preventing that is definitely a fight, but it is a worthy fight. In the Lord, I learned that I could be myself and rest my entire identity in Him.

Ellen and I talked about God together. I think it is really important for a high school relationship to have God in the center of it. Things get messy no matter what. But when you have a God-centered focus, you have perspective to help you make it through the ups and downs that come with any relationship. Fighting against temptation or any other struggle is much easier when you have something to fight for. Ellen and I committed to fight for purity and a relationship that glorified the Lord. We found strength in the Lord to not put up with the drama that usually comes with high school dating. You have to dare to be different, and you have to be ready to swim upstream. I can't say that it was always easy, but I wouldn't trade the way we did things for anything.

Knowing the Lord in high school really changed the way we dated. I continue to pray that He will change the way we live out our marriage as well. In high school, I was freaked out by people who were already talking about marriage. At 16, how could anyone really think that marriage was a practical topic of conversation? I'm sure there are right contexts for those conversations. But my teenage mind couldn't comprehend why we would talk about a future beyond going to homecoming together. Today, I'm grateful for that perspective. Ellen and I never really planned a future together. We definitely didn't start talking about marriage until I was thinking about proposing during Ellen's senior year of college. As a result, we got to be full-time high school students—not part-time students, part-time adults. Our four years together at Highland Park High School were awesome because we were excited about football games, school dances and pep rallies. I'm so glad we never got ahead of ourselves by trying to make future plans. When the time did come to think about getting engaged, we were ready. We knew the Lord was calling us to a life together because we had tasted how good it was just to be best friends.

On December 4, 2010, I stood at the end of a long aisle and waited for Ellen. Beside me stood 10 guys who had known me nearly my entire life. They had been my best friends since elementary school. That was a cool moment for me. I was getting ready to marry a girl I had grown up with, and I was surrounded by friends who had known me even longer. My situation is unusual in that my closest friends today are the ones I have known since I was young. I'm grateful to God for those guys. Proverbs 13:20 says, "He who walks with the wise grows wise, but a companion of fools suffers harm." These guys have walked through a lot of life with me, and we've shared wisdom and learned from stupid mistakes. But it has always been together.

While we were still in high school, Ellen and I decided to make sure that we kept strong friendships with other people. I needed my guys. She needed her girlfriends. Today, that continues to be a rich blessing in our marriage. We grew up with more than just each other. We grew up with our friends. Many teenagers develop tunnel vision and only hang out with their girlfriends or boyfriends. Almost unintentionally, Ellen and I didn't play by those rules. In fact, we rarely hung out just the two of us in high school. We were always with a group. Having people in your corner who know your relationship is so important. You need people who know you and point you to Christ. Those guys who stood by my side on December 4 know me well, because they were a part of my growing up, too. I'm so glad that we fought to keep those friendships a priority.

Ellen and I have lived a lot of life together—and we're still pretty young! We grew up holding on loosely. What I mean is that I loved having Ellen in my life, but I knew that she could never be everything to me. I couldn't look to her to fulfill me. Only Christ could do that. Ellen was a friend who pointed me toward God as we figured out life in high school. Part of growing up involves hitting bumps along the road. We certainly hit our fair share. But I look back on the way things unfolded and I wouldn't want it any other way. Growing up, especially in the Lord, is crucial. The blessing of my life is that I got to do it with my best friend.

# Break My Heart for What Breaks Yours

Ellen

**She looked at me with eyes that were deep and full of sorrow.** Without uttering a single word, she told me her life's story. In those dark brown eyes, I read things that would keep me awake at night. Parts of her story were so disturbing, I hoped to forget them by the next day. Yet at the same time, I wanted to remember each detail so that I could pray specifically for this child. She came around day after day. Each time, her facial expression softened when she saw me. Now using a few words, she would tell me about her home and what life was like for her. Her world sounded dark and joyless. We became fast friends that summer. Every time I think of Natasha, my heart breaks.

I met Patricia a few summers back. In 2009, I returned to Africa. The kids arrived at camp, and it wasn't hard to find Patricia. Before I knew it, she was running toward me! Without even pausing, she jumped into my hug and threw her arms around my neck. She didn't say anything until she pulled back and cupped my face in her tiny hands. "I missed you!" she exclaimed in beautiful, broken English. Her smile lit up an otherwise dreary day. As I remember her traumatic past, my heart breaks. But as I recall the grace of God in her life, my heart rejoices.

Diane had to grow up fast. Although she is only 12 years old, she helps care for her younger siblings. I often saw her stuffing her lunch into her pockets instead of eating it. When I asked her why she did that, she told me she was saving the food for her family. Diane met my sister one summer. For no apparent reason, she clung to my sister and started calling her "mother." Diane is one of thousands of children who are desperate for the love of a parent. My heart breaks over this reality.

The first time I met Hope, my world changed forever. At age 10, she had already seen more hurt, disease and death than I will likely see in my lifetime. Hope is a victim of HIV, and because of her affliction, her life will never be the same. Hope's story breaks my heart into a million pieces. I go to bed praying for her and wake up thinking about her. She has become the face behind my passion to carry the Lord's great hope to Africa.

When you pray for something big, and that prayer is God-centered, you had better be ready to receive a big, God-centered answer. I got myself into trouble when I prayed that the Lord would give me His heart for Africa. He heard that big, God-centered prayer and answered in extraordinary ways. I wasn't planning for my entire worldview to change, but God's response to my prayer overwhelmed me, and I will never be the same. Our prayers glorify God when we ask for something that only He can accomplish. Only the Lord could have turned my world upside down. Only the Lord could break my heart for children halfway around the world.

Have you ever felt like you are right in the middle of God's will for your life? There is a peace that surpasses all understanding and an excitement you can barely contain. When I am in Africa, I am confident that I am doing exactly what my heart was created for: worshiping the Lord and sharing His love with His children. Most of the children I have met in Africa are orphaned. AIDS and malnutrition are aggressively killing off their parents, relatives and friends. Their hurt is so deep, and the need is so great. In these devastating circumstances, only Jesus can bring the kind of hope that won't let these kids down.

Each year when I return, I have the privilege of seeing some of the same girls again and again. These girls learned at an early age to survive and not to trust anyone. They live in a world where enemies seem to be lurking around every corner. When children don't think anyone cares about them, they learn to fend for themselves. As several summers passed by and I kept returning, the Lord laid the foundations for deeper relationships and broke through emotional barriers. Over time, these girls have learned to trust me. They know that I am not a threat to them. So every year, they pour out to me their stories about life and home. It breaks my heart to realize that, on my own, I have so little to offer them. But I am reminded each time that what I do have to offer them—Jesus—can change their lives. I can give them love for a week, but Christ can provide His love for a lifetime. The Lord challenges my faith and humbles me by reminding me that He loves these kids more than I do or ever could. I am only there to point people to Him. So each day we talk about Jesus. He is the Person they really need. I grow more and more confident that the work He started in them while I was there will continue when I am gone.

The first time you hug a Zambian orphan, your life will be changed. Thankfully, that is my story. I am grateful to God that my life is different because of the children of Africa. Poverty in general is overwhelming. But when you know one particular person and can visualize one particular face, you realize that poverty is not just an impersonal blanket covering much of our world. It is real and it is personal. Each child affected by poverty has a story. When I first set foot in Zambia, I prayed that my heart would break for the things that break the Lord's heart. I also prayed that I would rejoice in the things that the Lord rejoices over.

As I traveled to Africa year after year, I began to pray for the time when Clayton would come with me. In 2011, God answered that specific prayer. I couldn't bear the thought of having half of my heart in Africa without Clayton knowing what it was all about. I knew that it would be logistically hard to pull it off with his baseball schedule, but I also believed that it was important for him to see what was happening in Zambia. I hated the thought of Clayton missing the Lord's spectacular work on the other side of the ocean. I wanted him to see what I saw. Although I am sure he was apprehensive about the whole experience, he jumped right in with me. He was eager to see what I had been talking about for so many years.

Within two hours of arriving in Africa, we were heading to the outskirts of the city, right into the slums. I was determined to find familiar faces from summers past. As I watched Clayton take it all in, I felt like I was seeing Africa for the first time all over again. He walked silently by my side, staring in disbelief at the surroundings. I remembered that exact feeling. I reached over and grabbed his hand, letting him know that I understood his thoughts and raw emotions. Real filth and poverty are overwhelming when you see them up close for the first time. The experience radically redefines your understanding of need.

A quiet afternoon vanished as the community began to stir with life. In tattered clothes, barefoot children came running. Some followed close behind us; others ran ahead to spread the news. They all looked at Clayton in awe. Most white people who visit are not that tall! One little guy fell in step with Clayton's long stride, walking close enough to reach up and touch him. Soon there was a crowd around us. We kept moving forward, and the children moved with us. In that moment, my two worlds collided. My husband was by my side, and the children who had changed my life five years earlier were all around us. I squeezed Clayton's hand to make sure he was still with me. He looked down at me and said, "This is incredible."

Our goal was to reach the home of a sweet girl named Miriam, whom I had met years before. We arrived at the humble home where Miriam lived with her mother, siblings and many other orphaned children. I was filled with joy at the sight of my young friend. As she crawled into my lap, we picked right back up where we had left off the summer before. She combed my hair, and then, licking her fingers, tried to rub the freckles off my arm, thinking they were dirt. Miriam's little sister, Jenny, took a particular interest in Clayton. She found her way up into his lap. He wrapped his arms around her, and she nestled into his chest, a picture of contentment. Clayton looked up at me with tears in his eyes. That was his moment. I had warned him that holding a Zambian orphan would change his life. Now he understood a little bit more of my heart. He felt the magnitude of what had been weighing on my spirit for years. Africa's blanket of poverty became so much more personal with Jenny in his arms.

After a long visit with Miriam's family, we prepared to leave. Clayton stood up, and Jenny dangled, her tiny arms still clinging tightly around his neck. He again looked at me in disbelief. "I don't think this is going to work," he laughed. Setting her down, he smiled and patted her on the head. Jenny stood still, just inches away from him, staring right up at his face. I don't think I'll ever forget that moment—and I'm pretty sure Clayton will never forget Jenny. Something changed in him that day. He picked her back up, squeezing her even tighter.

I continue to pray for a heart that breaks for the things that break the Lord's heart. I know it is a bold and dangerous prayer. Since I started praying, my heart aches for Africa in ways that I can hardly explain—and yet I consider it a rich gift to share God's heart for the things that He loves. When our hearts break for what breaks His, He calls us into action. We can no longer sit passively and hope for change. We have to be a part of the change. The Lord changed me when I started to realize that poverty is personal. As I could picture names, faces and stories, He gave me an incredible passion to share the gospel and my life. My heart breaks for Africa and the children that I think about every single day. I wouldn't have it any other way.

I pray that in your lifetime, you hear Him calling you to something bigger than yourself. I pray you find something that grabs your heart and fuels your spirit—something filled with great challenges and the blessing of His amazing grace. There are needs everywhere, not just in Africa. In your school, in your profession, in your hometown, or in a part of the world you've never heard of, there are people whose hurts and needs are vast. You can make a difference wherever He leads you to go (or stay). Just listen for His call, and then answer with all of your heart, never underestimating what the Lord can do through one person.

# GRACE FOR THE HUMBLE

Clayton

**Let's talk about "senioritis."** I had a serious case of it. I would wake up at 9 o'clock every morning, attend a short schedule of classes, and then take a long, leisurely lunch break with my seven buddies. We would play *Halo* and enjoy a homemade meal before racing in a dead sweat to make it to the stadium in time for practice. Clearly, I took my role as a senior in high school seriously. Baseball was the best part of that year. I lived for those moments in the legendary Highland Park stadium.

The lights at Scotland Yard were bright and hot. On a Texas summer day, they added to the already oppressive heat. The field sat right on Lovers Lane, a busy street that cuts the community in half. On game days, the moms would hang a sign from the bleachers announcing that there was a home game. The sign also served the purpose of warning cars about fly balls that might cruise over the dugouts and into the Lovers Lane traffic. The passage of time had worn on the stadium. Even with its new coat of blue paint, you could tell that it had been around for years and seen more than a few seasons. It was a proud moment when I first sat down in the home team's dugout. Playing for the Highland Park Scots varsity baseball team was a dream come true.

Some baseball seasons really stand out in my mind. In the past few years, I have seen things that I had only dreamed about seeing. Playing for the Dodgers has certainly been an incomparable experience. Still, I will remember my senior year baseball season for the rest of my life. My buddies and I had reached the pinnacle of sports at Highland Park. After years of playing on different Little League and select teams, we were finally all in the same uniform on the varsity team. For me, time stood still that season. I was with my best friends, doing what I most loved to do: play baseball. To this day, my senior baseball season remains one of my fondest memories.

Starting in our junior year of high school, guys started talking about college and the next four years of our lives. All of my friends were making lists of their top universities and dream colleges, but at that point, baseball was my focus. I had dropped out of football after freshman year to focus on my pitching—by which I really mean that I had gotten sick of playing center. Thank goodness my growth spurt finally kicked in. With my baby fat more or less gone and a few hairs sprouting on my chin, I started to think that maybe I could play baseball in college. Not only would I be living a dream, but I also saw baseball as a means to help pay for college. Baseball could give me the opportunity to go to college on a scholarship, which would be a blessing to my mom and me. So that was my goal: Play well enough to keep playing after high school.

Senior year finally arrived, and we could not have had a better group of guys. We played well enough to earn a spot in the playoffs. The stands were filled that season with our best friends, family and—much to my surprise—Major League scouts who started coming out to watch me throw. I tried not to pay too much attention to them, but it was hard to ignore them as they pulled out their radar guns every time I took the mound. I knew they were watching, and I made it my goal to perform well enough to keep them coming back. Sure enough, they did. By the time our season drew to a close, I was humbled to think that my baseball career wasn't over. I knew that I would at least get to play in college, and the scouts gave me hope that I might have a shot to be drafted. I found it hard to believe. I just tried to keep focusing on the team and what we were trying to accomplish.

I remember that last game as a Scot as if it took place yesterday. We were losing the game and on the verge of getting knocked out of the playoffs. Our fans were quiet and pensive as the innings ticked by. Slowly, I recognized the writing on the wall. We would lose this game, and that would be the end. As the last inning began, the guys were all standing in the dugout, ready to face the inevitable. As soon as the last pitch had been thrown, the visiting dugout emptied as our opponents' celebration spilled onto the field. Our guys stood together—like we had many times during our

12 years of playing baseball together. It was a weird moment for me. I knew that I'd have another shot to play. But I looked around and saw guys who had just played their last game. For all of us, it was the last game we would ever play together. Even though I was hopeful about another chapter, I knew that there would never be another season like this one with my best friends.

That was a humbling moment. It was humbling to lose when I was convinced we should be advancing. It was humbling to know that my story wasn't over. It was humbling to see our season and our baseball career together come to an end. I found encouragement in 1 Peter 5:5-7 during that time:

> All of you, clothe yourselves with humility toward one an-other, because, "God opposes the proud but gives grace to the humble." Humble yourselves, therefore, under God's mighty hand, that he may lift you up in due time. Cast all your anxiety on him because he cares for you.

Lessons in humility are always tough, especially when you are the one being humbled. The Lord used the end of my senior season to humble me. When things end abruptly, we don't necessarily re-alize the ramifications of the moment, but we always have a choice. We can become upset and bitter about what has happened. Or we can choose to receive it from the Lord's hand and accept it with hu-mility. Things will not always go the way we hope. I know exactly what that feels like. I would have given anything to play another game that season. However, that is not what the Lord had in mind.

When we humble ourselves before the Lord and His plan, we're in a better place. God intends to use all things for His glory and our joy. Losing a game could very well be in His will for us. He gives grace to the humble. However, in our pride, we often resist the Lord's will and set ourselves up for God to be against us. That doesn't sound like a good place to be.

Charles Spurgeon said something that makes a lot of sense to me: "We shall bring our Lord most glory if we get from Him much grace. If I have much faith, so that I can take God at His word . . . I shall greatly honor my Lord and King."[1] God gives us grace to handle tough moments so that we can bring Him glory. No two trials look the same. Maybe it's the end of baseball season. Maybe it's an illness. Maybe it's a breakup. Whatever our trials, I am convinced that God will give us grace to face them if we look to Him in humility. I wish I had known more about that during my senior year. I began to realize that year that the Lord uses all things—even a rough loss—to draw us closer to Him.

As we grow in humility, we learn to trust God when things don't go as we planned. We learn to believe that He is up to something bigger than the baseball season. He is more interested in what He is doing in our lives than in how we are performing in school and sports. When God gives us grace to be humble, we can see that losing a game isn't the end of the world. It may be a tough close to a great season, but God is up to something a whole lot bigger.

High school only lasts four years. Those were some of the best years of my life. I know that not everyone feels that way about high school. Maybe you're a high school student right now, and you can't wait to graduate. But those years in high school do offer great opportunities to mature as a person and to grow in the Lord. Cherish the time that you have there, and try to make the most of it. Don't hurry up to graduate. Enjoy where you are. Enjoy the people around you. You never know what the Lord is up to. Four years will fly by, and before you know it, you'll be playing your last game. In that moment, I hope you'll find the Lord to be enough. Because He is enough, even when you lose the last game, and your favorite season comes to an end. Walking with the Lord is even better than winning that last game. Life in Him is worth more than baseball. But we need a good dose of humility to see it that way. The Lord gives us grace to grow in humility. May we trust that what He has in store for us is better than anything we could ever imagine.

**Note**

1. Charles Spurgeon, *An All-Round Ministry* (Charleston, SC: BiblioBazaar, 2008), p. 190.

# 10

# FAMILY'S WHAT YOU MAKE IT

Clayton

**Ellen and I grew up in a unique community of friends and family.** The Highland Park area is relatively small, so everyone lives just blocks away from each other. I had a close-knit group of guys who were my best friends; we did everything together. During the school year, we would carpool to school and somehow end up in all of the same classes. Then we would spend the entire afternoon moving from house to house. We would eat dinner wherever we landed at dinnertime. Our moms became great friends as well and were always willing to feed the hungry pack of boys. We bounced around from meal to meal. Though I lived with just my mom, I felt like I had 10 different homes. We all felt that way. Home wasn't defined by the walls of a house—home was defined by the people we were with.

Summertime was the best. I probably slept at a different house every night. We would just crash wherever we found ourselves at the end of the day. Of course, we tended to land at the house that had the latest Xbox games. Summer was my favorite season of the year. With no school, we had plenty of time for pick-up games of basketball, and even more time to hang with friends. We were used to the heat of a Texas summer and took full advantage of the homes with swimming pools. For a lot of guys, summer was also a break from organized sports. For me, however, it was a chance to keep on playing with even greater focus. I joined summer baseball leagues and developed a community of friends and family all over the city of Dallas. Some of my closest friends were made on the baseball field during those summers. We went to different schools during the year—sometimes playing against each other's teams—but always found a way to reunite when summer came back around.

When I was growing up, I thought my family looked different from everyone else's. What I didn't realize then is that lots of people feel that way. There's not a formula for what a perfect family should look like. As I stumbled through middle school and high school, I decided that family is what you make it. According to my definition of family, I've been blessed immensely.

My family starts with my mom. She is an incredible person, and obviously I've known her for a long time. When I think about family, she is the first person who comes to mind. As an only child, I really had my mom's full attention. She walked with me through the ups and downs of growing up; she gave me direction and offered encouragement. It might have been easier for Mom and me to live somewhere else, but she thought it was worth it to be in Highland Park and made sure I could stay in the school district. As a result, I was able to play for a great baseball team and have the kind of exposure that would launch the next chapter of my baseball career. She never missed a game at Scotland Yard and could easily be spotted sitting in the stands, keeping track of every pitch and play. Mom made it work for us, though I know it wasn't easy at times. She sacrificed many things so that I could get a great education and stay close with my best friends. I know I wouldn't be where I am today without my mom. Her model of sacrifice still affects the way I want to give back to others. Family is what you make it, but it is also the gift of being born to such a great mother.

For me, family includes friends. I grew up a few doors down from Josh, the guy who would later stand next to me as the best man in my wedding. Josh and I did everything together. After school, I would go home with him and hang out until my mom got home from work. His family took me in as one of their own. My other buddies and their families were the same way. We traveled around like a troop of lost boys, making pit stops at homes along the way for snacks, Gatorade and video games. My buddies became my brothers. They teased me, and they laughed with me and at me. We did life together. Remember that great movie *The Sandlot*, about the neighborhood group of boys playing summer baseball together? That's how my life felt growing up. The community was our playground, and we biked the streets of our personal kingdom. God used those guys and their families to keep me on the right path. As I watched other families, I realized there wasn't a "right way" to be a family. Everyone else looked different, too. Seeing other families helped me to figure out who God wanted me to be. My "brothers" are still my best friends. They are my family.

It's an unusual situation when your in-laws play a huge role in raising you. Ellen's family was instrumental in shaping my definition of family. Because we started dating at age 14, our families played an integral role in our early relationship. If we wanted to hang out after school, we had to get someone to drive us. It was like having your parents chaperone a school dance, except it happened all the time. Humbling for a kid in high school, but I'm really thankful for how those years played out. Mom and I had a pretty quiet house. It was just the two of us and our faithful dogs, Nestle and Mike. So the Melson house was a trip for me. Chaos reigned, and everyone seemed to love it. Mama Melson could whip up a meal for 20 people faster than anyone I've ever met. I quickly became part of the practical jokes and friendly sibling rivalry. I wasn't born into a family with brothers and sisters, but they came along when I met the Melsons. At the time, I had voice cracks and a buzzed head for freshman football—complete with a #22 that almost looked like a swastika shaved on the back. Talk about a great first impression. The Melsons teased me relentlessly. As I watched Mr. Melson, I learned about being a selfless leader of the family. At that point, I never imagined that I would actually marry into their family. But as I look back, I can trace the Lord's goodness. Family's what you make it. The Melsons have been my family since I was a kid; it just became official when I married Ellen.

One of the things I love the most about baseball is that it is a team sport. The guys who share the bench and field with you become more than just teammates. They become family. One year, the Highland Park baseball team chose the slogan "Band of Brothers." That's exactly how I felt. Shared experiences often create meaningful relationships. Winning and losing with my teammates forged a strong bond. Our parents traded off carpools and sat in the stands together. Whenever you made a good play, you heard more than just your own mom cheering. Every team I've played on has been a family to me. It has become a big family, because baseball has been a part of my life since I can remember. I'm so thankful for my baseball family that includes friends, coaches and parents. As I continue to play today, I feel like they are still calling me forward to be the man God wants me to be.

Most recently, a new family started when I married Ellen. We bring different definitions of the word "family" to this new chapter. Ellen comes from a loud and large family. She actually knows her second and third cousins. I come from a quieter family where most of the members are not blood-related. Despite our different backgrounds, we agree on several things that we want to incorporate into our new family. Sunday night dinners are always important, and our home will feature a revolving door of people coming and going. Dogs are to be treated like humans, and card games are to be taken very seriously. We'll play pranks and watch *The Office* before going to sleep. The last activity of the day will be praying together. We have an idea of what our family will look like. But the best part is figuring it out together one day at a time.

I was wrong when I thought that family had to look a certain way. Sure, genes and last names and family trees have something to do with it, but family is so much more than that. In our culture today, families follow lots of different models. Some people grow up with two parents and some grow up with one. Many people don't even know their biological parents. I continue to believe that family is what you make it. At the end of the day, relationships are what really matter. I am learning even now that relationships are vital to a fulfilling life in Christ. The Lord didn't intend for us to do life by ourselves. He wants us to be in community with other believers. I love playing baseball. But even baseball would be miserable if it weren't for relationships. Without meaningful friendships, even the best job in the world can be unbearable.

I don't have an average family. I'll bet you feel the same way. The definition of a family is different for everyone. I've heard it said that it takes a village to raise a kid. I believe it! I have a large family back home in Texas—people who have loved and supported me since before I can remember. From Mom and the Melsons to my long-time friends and teammates, family is as narrow as a bloodline and as wide as a community of love and support. These people welcome me home after a long season away, and old relationships pick up right where they left off. Families make sacrifices and do whatever it takes to help us become the people the Lord made us to be. My definition of family is very loose: Family's what you make it. It's pretty sweet when you realize that God has blessed you with a huge family.

# 11

## THE PURSUIT OF PASSION

Ellen

**In a high school cafeteria, it's all about blending in.** No one wants to stand out or, heaven forbid, do something to draw the wrong kind of attention. There is just something about a school cafeteria that brings out all our random insecurities. You grab your lunch. You sit down at your usual table, praying you don't slip on a greasy French fry or have your skirt tucked in your underwear. The goal: Just try to make it to your seat with dignity. If you can, add a little bit of swagger. You sit with the same people you always sit with—and then you leave. Whew, deep breath—a flawless lunch. No one in his right mind would do something to draw direct attention. That's why it caught me off guard when my friend Will stood up on a table in the middle of fourth-period lunch one day.

His whistle pierced the air, bringing all conversations to a halt. Everyone turned to see what the commotion was all about. I held my breath, terrified for Will—shocked that he would voluntarily put himself in such an uncomfortable position. Interestingly, the attention didn't appear to bother him. In fact, he seemed pleased to have every eye in the cafeteria on him. The whole scene was strange. Conversations turned to whispers. Will whistled again, and then even the murmurs fell silent. "Guys, what are we doing here? What are we doing with our lives?" he exclaimed. I sat in disbelief at his bravery. No one said a word. They leaned in to hear what else he was going to say. He talked about living for the Lord and finding purpose in Him. With everyone in the cafeteria listening, Will challenged his peers to consider faith and the thought that God had great purpose for our lives.

In a high school where most students professed to be Christians, no one ever talked about it. Certainly no one stood on a table and talked about faith in the middle of lunch. Will shared from his heart and charged us to think about life and making an impact.

He had a captive audience for only a few brief moments, but he made his point. He hopped off the table and went on with his day, walking out of the cafeteria while the rest of us stood speechless. Activity and conversation paused. No one knew how to respond to what had just happened. One of our peers had made an incredibly brave, bold move. Jaws had dropped. But Will didn't care. He seemed confident, intent on sharing his message with the world. I don't think Will had any idea at the time how much that moment would mean for so many people, including me. His courage and conviction left a lasting impression. I still think about that day. At a young age, when most of us were thinking only about Friday night plans and trying to blend in, Will was thinking about doing something spectacular with his life. He was thinking about making a lasting impact and living for the Lord.

Today, Will is a successful filmmaker, bringing glory to God as he uses his creativity and talent to produce films. Even in high school, I knew that there was something different about him. He talked about purpose in life because he really believed that we all have one. Will was brave enough to raise the subject in a crowded cafeteria of his peers. He put words to questions that we all had in the back of our minds: "What is my purpose? How do I make sure that my life has meaning?" Will took a bold step that day. It's easy to think that high school is all about us. If we are not careful, everything we do and think can become self-centered. If we want to get over ourselves, we have to want to live for something more. Will took the risk of embarrassment in front of friends to wake us up to that possibility. By God's grace, he wanted to live with purpose—and he wanted others to fight for the same thing. He had a rare perspective in high school—a perspective that drew his focus away from himself and onto the Lord. Will and I still stay in touch. I'm really proud to call him a friend.

The Lord intends for His children to have an impact right where they are. I wish I had known that sooner. When I heard Will talking about it, I was intrigued. Everyone has a place. Everyone has a greater purpose. We waste so much time thinking that one day we'll have purpose—but not today. We set up unrealistic expectations for ourselves. We think that we have to achieve a certain goal or reach a certain status before we can do anything that really matters. Some people will spend a lifetime looking for significance and their life's purpose. But the amazing thing is that we all have purpose right now, right where we are planted. We don't have to wait for the next chapter of our lives to begin a life of great purpose. The Lord intends for us to live with that purpose now. Will caught onto that vision in high school. He knew that the way he lived his life between his freshman and senior years really mattered.

Most of us think that someone else will be the one to have great impact. We think, *Someone will surely change the world—but it won't be me. My purpose could never be that important.* But what if *we* were the ones to change the world? What if *we* were the ones to have incredible impact? I remember that when I first started dreaming about Africa in eighth grade, I thought someone else could go. Someone more equipped could go to Africa and do extraordinary things for the sick, impoverished and lost. There were plenty of full-time missionaries over there who could do a better job than I could! Surely the Lord had a long list of people to send before He would ever need me.

Will's declaration in the cafeteria that day got me thinking about my purpose. What if my purpose *was* to go to Africa? What if the Lord really could do something through me? Just a year later, I crossed the ocean and landed in Africa. If I had believed the lies in my head that the Lord didn't have a purpose for me in Africa, I never would have gone. I would have missed one of the greatest blessings in my life. Now I can't imagine my life without the children of Zambia. The devil wants us to believe that we don't have a purpose. Nothing could be further from the truth. The Lord has a specific purpose for each of us, and we are never too young to start thinking about it.

Purpose begins right where we are. The Lord brings people and circumstances into our lives with great intention. Don't wait for the next chapter of your life to consider the Lord's purpose for you. It's happening right now, right where you are. Whether you are in the middle of a tough season or a joyful one, the Lord is showing you something—even if you can't see what it is until you are a little further down the road. If we all realized that we have a purpose and decided we want to make an impact right where we are, the world would look completely different. Have you ever thought about that? Anyone, anywhere can make an impact—in a high school, in a friend group, in extracurricular activities. You can have impact today.

When we are right in the middle of what God calls us to do, we feel His pleasure. I learn so much about this from watching Clayton. God has called him to play baseball, and he loves it so much. The classic movie *Chariots of Fire* tells a powerful story about God's purpose and human pleasure colliding. Every great sports figure can relate to Eric Liddell, the main character of the movie. Eric is an Olympic runner who was born into a missionary family. Instead of following his family to the mission field, Eric decides to pursue his passion for running. He truly believes that it is part of God's purpose for him. His sister challenges him to reconsider his decision. She thinks he should give up his running and join the family in China. Eric's answer is profound: "I believe God made me for a purpose, but He also made me fast. And when I run, I feel His pleasure." Eric expresses something we all long to find: a way to fulfill our purpose with great pleasure. Eric Liddell glorified the Lord in his running, and later he would glorify the Lord as a missionary in China, too. When we run in the paths the Lord has for us, we feel His pleasure.

Clayton's senior year at Highland Park fit that description perfectly. It was a sweet season of life for him—a time when he felt the pleasure of God because he was doing what he was made to do: play baseball. Even looking back today, he remembers that season as an incredible collision of joy and purpose. Baseball was his love. Nothing could compare with the joy of getting to play it with his best friends. On a typical day, the guys would get out of school and spend the afternoon playing *Super Smash Brothers* on Nintendo until they were late to baseball practice. They always had a competition to see who could make it to the field first without getting in trouble. I remember walking by practice one afternoon on the way to my car. They were all laughing, making fun of each other, and playing baseball. They were in their element—joyful and carefree— and they still talk about those "glory days." In some ways, not much has changed since senior year. The boys still get together to play *Smash Brothers* (whatever that is). They still throw the baseball around and occasionally peg someone in the stomach for fun. For as long as I can remember, Clayton has loved baseball. It has never been work for him. It's always been his joy and passion.

When Clayton plays baseball, he feels the pleasure of God. When I love on God's children in Africa, I feel His pleasure. We experience great joy when we do what God made us to do. In the middle of God's purpose, we find His pleasure. Or maybe you can think about it the other way around. Maybe your greatest joy will help you find God's purpose for you. What do you love the most? Perhaps that is exactly where God wants to use you. My friend Will talked about finding purpose when we were all wondering the same thing. He suggested that we start looking where God had us at that moment—in high school. I'm so glad Will was bold enough to stand out and look different in the middle of a high school cafeteria. He got me thinking about purpose. The idea of going to Africa was already on my mind. The Lord used the bravery of a friend to make me consider that living out my dream was possible. He also encouraged me to believe that I had purpose, even as a student in high school. You don't have to wait for something big to happen in your life. Purpose begins when we realize that the Lord is at work in us right here, right now.

# 12

## THAT CAN'T BE RIGHT

Clayton

**Have you ever dreamed about a life-changing moment?** Have you ever seen it coming from a mile away? Has that moment ever surprised you out of nowhere? Sometimes you realize such a moment is approaching. Other times, one of them sneaks up on you, and suddenly your life is different. Maybe there's a moment you've dreamed about for your whole life. The realistic voice in you says, "It will never happen," but somewhere in your heart, there's a crazy hope that holds on to the dream. "It just might happen after all."

I had turned 18 in March of that year. We had just walked the stage as graduates of Highland Park High School. College was in sight for most of us. I had signed with Texas A&M University to play baseball on scholarship. I loved the coach and the program, and Ellen was heading to A&M, too. Those were enough reasons for me to agree to be an Aggie. So that was my plan on the day I received my diploma.

Our senior baseball season had ended in defeat, but the year had been about so much more than wins and losses. I still had many incredible memories. During my junior year, I had thought that I might get to play baseball in college. By senior year, the opportunities were more than I could have dreamed. Still, I worried about the future and finances. I didn't know how we were going to make things work. I had so much to figure out, and many times I just assumed nothing significant would ever come my way. Anxiety became a battle for me as I considered the future. If only I had known then how much the Lord would provide. Philippians 4:6-7 raced repeatedly through my mind—and over time, I began to believe it:

> Do not be anxious about anything, but in everything, by prayer and petition, with thanksgiving, present your requests to God. And the peace of God, which transcends all

understanding, will guard your hearts and your minds in Christ Jesus.

During my senior season, the Lord's presence became more real in my life than ever before. He took away all of my anxieties about finances and making things work, replacing them with a peace that surpassed my understanding. I didn't have things figured out, but I heard the Lord telling me to relax and to trust Him. He answered my questions and prayers, one at a time. People started taking notice of me on the pitching mound. Scouts showed up for games and hung around to talk to me afterwards. It was surreal. At the time, I didn't think the Lord had any idea how much I was struggling to trust Him with the future. But looking back now, I see God's tight grip on my life. He had a firm hold on me and answered every question and doubt that I threw His way. God's grace to me in that season was really remarkable. The Lord taught me that He is worthy of my full trust and able to do more than I could imagine. I wish I had realized that sooner; if I had, I wouldn't have gotten so stressed every time life got rough in high school.

When the Major League draft became more than just a possibility, agents started seeking my attention. I was blessed to land in the hands of J.D. Smart from Hendricks Sports Management in Houston. J.D. and I became fast friends, and I looked to him to walk me through the draft and other possibilities. As an 18-year-old kid who had barely left Texas, I needed all the help I could get.

Two weeks before draft day, I still had my sights set on Texas A&M, hesitant to believe that the draft could really present an opportunity that would change my plans. J.D. was confident that something would come my way, and he took me to lunch to discuss the process and potential options. I had so many thoughts in the back of mind, one of which was: *Will it even be worth it to sign a contract?* I still doubted that I could play baseball and actually make enough money to call it a career. Dreams don't always play out the way we hope.

J.D. and I went to Chips, a Dallas establishment known for great burgers. I sat hunched over my burger, listening to J.D. as he explained the draft process. Then he paused, catching my attention. "How much money would it take for you to sign a contract?" he asked.

I laughed and shook my head. "Enough to cover the cost of this lunch," I replied. That was pretty close to the truth. I wasn't looking to get rich. After a long pause, J.D. got very serious and told me that I had the potential to sign a contract for an amount of money that blew me away. Burger still in hand, I lost my breath, and my eyes filled with tears. I set down my burger and put my head in my hands. "That can't be right. That can't be right," was all I could manage to say. As I looked back up at J.D., all sorts of emotions washed over me. What he had just told me was astounding and humbling. The Lord's grace in my life left me speechless.

I left that lunch weak in the knees, but with a new assurance that the Lord would provide. After years of worrying about how we would make ends meet, I was watching the Lord cover my bases many times over.

June 6, 2006, finally arrived. Draft day. Ellen and all my close friends came over to our house to wait and see what the day would hold. We had the TV on, the computer streaming breaking news, and a phone nearby, just in case a call came. J.D. had walked me through the proceedings and how to handle things if and when that phone rang. The first round of the draft began, and teams selected players with the first six picks. Overall pick number seven was next. Then came one of those life-changing moments. The phone rang. The Los Angeles Dodgers called to say that they would be drafting me with the next pick. That phone call was the most nerve-racking and exciting call I have ever received. I tried to remain calm and collected, but a voice crack every other sentence surely gave me away. Everything inside of me wanted to just let loose and celebrate with my family and friends—which I did as soon as I had hung up the phone. The whole room erupted in excitement as the Lord's will unfolded, making me an L.A. Dodger. I knew that it would be a long road ahead. I had my work cut out for me, but I also knew that this was a "dream come true" moment that I would never forget.

God's goodness is sometimes hard to grasp. When I worried if He would ever show up, He was already there. I didn't know it as a high-schooler, but God had hemmed me in, behind and before, covering everything that I needed. You might be tempted to believe that the Lord is not in control, or that He has forgotten to take care of you. I know what that's like. But I also know what it's like to realize that He was there the whole time, weaving things together in a way that would one day blow my mind.

When that moment came, I held my head in my hands and said, "That can't be right." God's goodness is that astonishing, and we can rely on Him always being good. In high school, the Lord provided more than I needed, and He taught me to trust Him. I am amazed that He has allowed me to live my dream, and I'm even more amazed that He was so patient with an anxious kid who didn't really believe that His grace would be more than enough.

# 13

# WELCOME TO
# THE MINOR LEAGUES

Clayton

**The other guys were all hanging in the main room watching TV.** They had no idea what I was up to. We were on a road trip, all staying on the tenth floor of a high-rise hotel in the middle of the city. I was having the time of my life. They started yelling at me from the other room, wondering what I was doing with the water running in the bathroom. "Don't worry about it," I responded, laughing to myself. They weren't expecting my next move. All of a sudden, I barreled through the room with a full load of water balloons. Throwing back the balcony door, I started launching balloons toward the street below. "Let's get 'em!" I yelled. The guys were initially dumbfounded, but then quickly joined in the air raid. As each balloon splattered against the pavement or a passing car, we'd duck out of sight. I could barely catch my breath from laughing. The raid was ridiculous—borderline stupid. We could have gotten in a lot of trouble. But that's what happens when you give a bunch of young guys the afternoon off after a game. We worked hard—and we played hard, too. There is something about the Minor Leagues that turns men into overgrown boys. It's awesome.

A day before the MLB draft, all I had known was that I could land in any number of cities around the country. I couldn't even guess where I might end up. Draft day finally came, and suddenly my entire world turned and focused on a new city and a new team: the Los Angeles Dodgers. I had never been to California, but I knew enough about it to think the journey ahead would be pretty sweet. A few days later, I was packing up to head to Los Angeles. It's amazing how much your life can change in a week.

It felt like going to college for me. Ellen and my buddies were heading to various universities in the fall. So I decided to think of L.A. as the next practical step for me . . . kind of like college was for everyone else. Not really knowing what to pack, I loaded my bag with a whole assortment of things. I was scheduled to go to Los Angeles first, so I pulled out my one suit and some nice clothes to make a good first impression. It was weird saying goodbye to my mom and friends, not really knowing when I'd be back home. Ellen was leaving for summer school around the same time. It helped that we both had places to be. I didn't feel like I was leaving her behind, because I knew she had stuff to do as well.

Even the plane flight was exciting. I could hardly believe that this all was happening. When I landed in L.A., I was introduced to Preston Mattingly. We were both Dodger draft picks, and I was grateful to have someone else diving in with me. Preston's dad had been a great player for the Yankees, so he was a little more comfortable in this world than I was. I felt like a fish out of water, but I was eager to figure it all out. We were picked up at the airport and rode in a nice, black car to Dodger Stadium, where we officially signed our contracts. We were also given a tour of the clubhouse, field and offices. The team made us feel like royalty.

For the next couple of days, we were shown around the city and introduced to baseball legends like Tommy Lasorda. His personality is larger than life. He told us story after story of his time with the Dodgers, which included winning two World Series championships as the manager. We toured the press box, and I got to shake hands with the "Voice of the Dodgers," Mr. Vin Scully. He has been the official broadcaster for the team for 62 years—the longest tenure of any professional sports broadcaster with a single team. I loved that this club was so rich with tradition and history. I couldn't believe I got to be a part of it. I felt undeserving of the amazing opportunity I'd been given. I was walking around in my dream, surrounded by baseball legends I had written book reports about as a kid.

The weekend in Los Angeles was incredible. I thought to myself that this baseball life could be pretty sweet. I felt so welcomed by the organization, and I was ready to get to work. Preston and I flew to Vero Beach, Florida, where we joined the Rookie Ball League of the Dodgers. My time in L.A. had me thinking that my new life would be fairly plush. Not that I was used to that kind of living. It just seemed as though that's how this baseball world rolled. So I was a little surprised when we were picked up by a van and driven to the middle-of-nowhere Florida, to a sleepy little town. Driving through Vero Beach, I noticed how quiet the town was—nothing like the chaos of Los Angeles. Street signs were worn with age and all had "Dodgertown" painted on them. This was my first experience in a baseball town—a place that lived and breathed summer baseball. The van dropped us off at a building that looked like an old dorm. Home sweet home.

Preston and I were sent in different directions. I went to my room and met the guy who had been assigned to be my roommate for the next two months. The dorm room looked like a motel—two beds tossed into one big room. "Wow," I thought. Welcome to the Minor Leagues. This was way different from the week before. But honestly, the circumstances at Vero Beach fit me like a glove. I was in my element. Simple felt more like home to me. I spent the next two months playing Rookie Ball at Vero Beach. Ellen's family, vacationing a few hours up the coast, came down for a visit. It was nice to have a taste of home, and to be reminded that I wasn't fighting for this dream without the support of family and friends. I quickly settled into the routine of playing baseball every day and hanging with the guys at night. Even though we were from all over the country, we all had one thing in common—baseball.

The weird thing about the Minor Leagues is that you never feel like you're in control of any part of your life. When you play, where you live, when (or if) you get moved up to the next level—other people make those decisions for you. After my first season in Vero Beach, I was sent to start all over again as a Great Lakes Loon in Midland, Michigan. This time, I was dropped off at a hotel and given three days to find a place to live and get ready for the season. Thankfully, there were a few other guys in the same boat. We stumbled upon some apartments near the field. None of my teammates came from anywhere near Midland. I had a funny moment when I realized I was standing somewhere in Michigan, and I thought, *What am I doing here?* Our bizarre circumstances led to instant bonding among the guys. We all laughed as we walked into a completely bare apartment. Luckily, we found the perfect solution to furnish our home—a nearby Walmart. We went in together and bought air mattresses, a patio table and chairs, a few beanbags, and a sweet TV. We were set. That's how we lived for four months. We only returned to Walmart three times during our stay in Midland—to replace air mattresses when they popped.

For me, the Minor Leagues were my college experience. My group of friends growing up was really tight. I had doubted that I'd ever find friends like that again. But the guys I met in Midland came awfully close. We held wrestling matches and played Nintendo 64 until our fingers had blisters. Playing baseball with this group was awesome. It was like starting over again, but feeling right at home at the same time. Those four months flew by. Ellen came out to visit a few times and was horrified by our living arrangements. But it was perfect for us. A few of the other guys had girlfriends who visited as well. That was the first time Ellen and I felt like we had a baseball family. Even though those guys are playing for different teams now, there's something about those months in Midland that still ties us together. When we get together, we can pick up right where we left off. I am immensely grateful for my time in places like Midland and Vero Beach.

I grew so much in my confidence and in my faith during my time in the Minors. I was beginning a new chapter, far away from everything that had been home to me. I thought about the Lord in new ways and found myself more dependent on my time with Him. I discovered that faith in God really could hold me up when things seemed so unsure. Playing in the Minor Leagues was really humbling for me. I had to work hard to see results. Those years also allowed me to grow up alongside guys who were the same age as me. I was only 18 years old and had a lot to learn. Sometimes the Lord surprises you. He knew that I needed those two years of figuring things out in the Minors. He also knew that I would need a baseball family—guys who would walk with me through the ups and downs of playing baseball and even encourage me in my faith. I didn't know that I needed that experience. But God did.

There were plenty of moments during those two years that reminded me I was in the Minors. When I was sleeping on a deflated air mattress in an empty apartment, I couldn't help but laugh to myself. Road trips always caused me to think about my dream of getting to play in the Majors. We would travel to places like Clinton, Iowa. Driving through the night, I would lie down on the dirty bus floor to get a few hours of sleep. I hadn't imagined sleeping on the floor of a bus, but that was part of living out my dream of playing baseball. As long as I got to do that, I figured things were turning out pretty well. I hoped that the coming years would be even better, but I didn't want to rush it. I needed that time to work hard and improve as a player. I needed that time to be 18 years old. I never knew when the Dodgers might move me up or down, but I didn't want to stress about that. I just tried to enjoy where the Lord had me. I met some of my best friends. I worked on my pitching. I played some great practical jokes. Those were some of the best years of my life.

# 14

## BY THE GRACE OF GOD, I AM WHAT I AM

Ellen

**When I was growing up, vacations with my family were legendary.** We never really took an "ordinary" trip. I recall one trip in particular: We packed a large bus full of 18 family members wearing matching T-shirts, visors and fanny packs. I'm not kidding. We toured just about every national park in the western United States and overwhelmed every picnic area in our path. We spent three full weeks together on "The Great Western Trip." Well, we were together most of the time. One day we accidentally left one of my uncles behind in Death Valley. Thirty minutes down the road, we stopped at a scenic overlook and realized we didn't have our official photographer. We made it back for Uncle Jeff, but not before he found the Death Valley post office to send a postcard to my parents, just in case he didn't make it out alive. Another day, my mom wanted to teach us kids a lesson about the pitfalls of gambling. We all stood around and watched as she dropped a quarter into a slot machine in Vegas. Lights flashed and sirens blared as Mom won $1,500 with one quarter. Not sure we learned that lesson.

My family consisted of my parents and four kids—my older brother, Jed; my older sister, Ann; me; and my younger brother, John. Mom and Dad would move mountains for us if they could, and there was never a day that I didn't know how much they loved me. I was born and raised in Dallas, Texas, and I only remember living in one house my entire childhood. I grew up thinking that everyone was born into a loving, Christian family. We never missed a Sunday at church and would pray before meals as a family. I came to know Christ as my Savior at a summer camp when I was eight years old. That seemed pretty typical to me, too. I never gave the "normalcy" of my life much thought until I left the country.

In Africa, I met boys and girls whose stories were vastly different from mine. Many knew only one of their parents. Even more didn't know either of their parents. Orphans in Zambia are for the most part unloved and unwanted. Suddenly, I realized how rare it is to have a mom and dad living under the same roof. By the world's standards, I was born healthy. Many children in Africa don't share that experience. For me, AIDS was just an epidemic I heard about in school. But for these children, it was an everyday reality. AIDS might have taken their parents or siblings. They themselves might have been born with it. They might have done everything they could to avoid contracting it. But they couldn't escape it.

I learned quickly that many of the African children I met had never heard of Jesus. When I got to talk with them, John 3:16 rolled off my tongue like it had been etched in my mind forever: "For God so loved the world that he gave his one and only Son, that whoever believes in him shall not perish but have eternal life." To the children of Zambia, the thought of a heavenly Father was completely foreign. A truth that I had taken for granted was an earthshaking revelation for these kids. Everything in my life that had seemed so typical now became precious and uncommon. God used the people of Zambia to make me more aware of His grace in my life.

The apostle Paul had a deep understanding of who he really was. In his letter to the Corinthians, he told the believers, "By the grace of God I am what I am, and his grace to me was not without effect. No, I worked harder than all of them—yet not I, but the grace of God that was with me" (1 Cor. 15:10). Jesus stopped Paul in his tracks. After once living to persecute and destroy Christ's Church, Paul knew he couldn't take credit for the radical change in his life. He wasn't good enough or powerful enough to save or change himself. By the grace of God, Paul was who he was. He used to be a man defined by all the things he did as a Pharisee, but now he was a man defined by the grace God had lavished on him. A loving, merciful God had sought him out and turned him around. There was no other explanation for his life. By the grace of God, he was a changed man!

As I thought about Paul's words, I realized that they described me as well. It was no mistake that God placed me in a big Texas family that would point me to Jesus at an early age. That was grace! Before I had a chance to think about Jesus, He was already at work in my heart. Before I knew my need for a Savior, He knew that I needed Him. I can get overwhelmed thinking about the number of children in Africa who don't know the Lord. But then I remember: He knows them. He knows what they need. He knows every hair on their heads. He knows everything about them, and He is already at work in their hearts. It's a comforting thing to know that the Lord's grace runs ahead of us and chases after us.

We can't forget the Lord's sovereign hand over our lives. He places each of us in a certain family, in a specific place on the globe, and He gives every one of us a life with great purpose. When I consider the lives of the precious children in Zambia, I don't think they're less fortunate than I am. I have more in the way of material blessings, but that doesn't always make things better in the end. A lot of times, the things we call "blessings" end up distracting us from what life is really all about. The orphans in Zambia have taught me so much about faith. They understand need and desperation so much better than I do. When they hear the good news that God loves them, they respond with a joy that takes my breath away. I don't think my life is better—it's just different. I see how the Lord has been intentional in my life, so I can trust His purpose in their lives as well. I also know that part of God's purpose for me is to go and tell them about this Jesus who has changed my life. The Lord gives me an opportunity to tell them about Him, and then I get to watch as He opens their eyes to see His grace for themselves.

God's grace in our lives doesn't depend on what we do. It depends on what Jesus did. We don't receive grace because we deserve it or because we know how much we need it. God loves us regardless of our ability to love Him back. When I reflect on my life, I see how true that is. As a child, I didn't know how much I needed God. But He was there and already at work. That is grace.

By God's grace, I have a heart for Africa. By God's grace, Clayton can really throw a baseball. We're hopeful that we can spend a lifetime figuring out what those two things mean and how to live them out for God's glory. That's how we choose to see the gifts we've been given. Perspective is a beautiful thing. When we begin to see people, things and circumstances through the lenses of God's grace, we can't help but notice His goodness. Sometimes the Lord decides to take us somewhere unfamiliar to tear down the walls of our all-too-familiar life. God has used my trips to Africa to help me see His hand at work in my life and in the lives of others. From the other side of the world, the Lord's grace in my life looked overwhelmingly different. I could see my life with new eyes. God has been faithful to me for a lifetime. I see His gracious hand all over the place! The more I see it, the more I long to change my focus to the things that are most important. Every time I go to Africa, I come home wanting to be different.

By the grace of God, I am what I am, but I know He's not finished with me yet. The Lord has used everything in my life up to this point to draw me to Himself. The more I look back, the more my confidence in His grace grows. So I have incredible hope for the future. My life is not an accident. The Lord knew that I would be part of a family that takes legendary vacations. He knew that we'd all come up with nicknames for each other that make life really confusing for everyone else. He knew that people like Shush, Lulu, Pudge, Dee, Peach, Nee Nee and Tink would be part of His plan. None of this was by chance. It was all grace. All that I have, all that I am and all that I hope to be—it's all because of God's grace.

# 15

# DARING TO BE DIFFERENT

Clayton

**It's never easy to look different, but at least there's comfort in knowing we're not alone.** I'm pretty sure we've all had moments when we just knew we didn't quite fit in with the people around us—especially during those awkward teenage years. Ellen and I were no exceptions. For instance, in middle school Ellen wore headgear that would attach to her braces with a lightning bolt down the head strap. We ran across it recently, and I paid her $10 to prove that it still fit. Personally, I have always been larger than average for a guy my age. Although it has turned out okay, and I am now grateful for my size, it wasn't always easy being the big kid.

Josh was my best friend growing up, and he's always been half my size, with twice as much muscle. We grew up just a couple doors down from each other, so we rode our bikes to elementary school together every day. One year, we had the brilliant idea of putting pegs on my bike for Josh to ride with me to and from school. My competitive nature came out at an early age, and I would do anything to beat Josh in a race (which never happened). One afternoon, we were sprinting to the bike after school when I ran into a doorframe and promptly blacked out. It took all Josh's might to get me to my feet. I staggered to the bike rack with the world still spinning around me. Josh tried to pedal home with me on the pegs, but I wasn't exactly a light load. So I had to pedal while Josh steered my shoulders to lead us in a straight line. We later found out that I had a minor concussion. Looking different has always been rough, but the funny stories make the pain well worth it.

Growing up in Highland Park, looking different wasn't necessarily a good thing. Life was easier if you could blend in with everyone else. For a lot of people at my high school, being a Christian was run of the mill. Not only was Christianity widely accepted, but it also was the cool thing to be a Christian—a nominal one, anyway. People claimed to follow Jesus and then lived however they wanted. They didn't want their Christianity to get in the way of having a good time. I grew a lot in my faith during high school, but I also played the game of fitting in. My faith was more personal than public. It's still that way. I guess people could look at my life and make assumptions. My faith is something that I take very seriously but keep very private.

In high school, I was blessed with a group of friends who shared the values I held. We decided early on that we wanted to make the most of our four years at Highland Park. Like everyone else, we wanted to have fun on the weekends, but we wanted to do it differently. We enjoyed going to parties, but we would usually end the night at the Dickensons' playing basketball or at Ellen's house with the chocolate fountain. We decided not to drink alcohol, but we felt comfortable being friends with those who did. We didn't want to separate ourselves completely from people who were different from us. We had each other, and we were comfortable in our own shoes. Together, we found a way to make the most of our four years at Highland Park. We dared to be different, and we loved every minute of it.

Then we all graduated. My friends took off for college, and I jumped into baseball. While Ellen enjoyed the typical college life at Texas A&M University, I found myself in the Middle of Nowhere, America, trying to make a career out of playing baseball. I moved away from home for the first time. I met guys from all over the place. Some were even from other countries, like Venezuela and the Dominican Republic. Once again, I found myself looking different from the people around me. Except that for the first time, my peers were all the same size as me—XXL. Now, though, I was in a giant blender of backgrounds and beliefs. In many ways, that was refreshing. In other ways, it could be overwhelming. Suddenly, I was sharing a room with guys, and I didn't know much more than their first names. I could only assume that they loved baseball as much as I did. Eventually, we all became friends. But I'll never forget those first few weeks of feeling a little out of place.

The Minor Leagues opened up so many opportunities for me. Obviously, the baseball opportunities were awesome. But more than that, the Minors offered a crash course in understanding other people. I had never been in a place where people looked really different from one another. When you spend your entire childhood in the same small community, you mostly look like everyone else. When all you know is a little neighborhood in Dallas, Texas, Minor League Baseball looks really different. As I got to know players from across the country and around the world, I realized how much I needed to figure out who I was.

I had never thought of my faith as something that made me look different. For the first time, I started to see that it was. Back home, we all went to church together on Sunday and met for a Bible study on Tuesday nights. In the Minors, my world changed really quickly, so I tried to hang on to the things that made sense to me. Even though I didn't pack much, I brought my Bible and a devotional book. Every day, I tried to spend time with the Lord—and I guess that looked unusual to some guys. People start asking questions when a life looks different from whatever they think is normal. Guys asked me, "What are you reading? Why are you reading that?"—and for the first time, I had to explain my faith. I remember reading 1 Peter 3:15: "But in your hearts set apart Christ as Lord. Always be prepared to give an answer to everyone who asks you to give the reason for the hope that you have. But do this with gentleness and respect." I started to see that I had a different hope than many of the people around me. If I looked different, people were going to ask why, and I wanted to be ready to answer questions about my faith.

Simple questions opened up big doors of opportunity to share my faith with others. One late afternoon, I was standing in the outfield, shagging fly balls during a batting practice. One of my buddies came up to me and started a casual conversation. He was curious about how I talked. I've never been one to use foul language, and I guess that caught his attention. He pointed out that I seemed to go out of my way to say things less offensively. "Why not just cuss?" he asked. "What's the big deal?" I had never thought about that before. It quickly became apparent that these moments were opportunities to talk about the Lord. For the most part, conversations in the outfield were never too complex. But they did give me chances to share about the Lord, His influence on my life, and even my language. Sometimes the conversations ended there, but other times they went deeper.

The Lord's grace leads us to live in a way that looks different to others. It makes sense. If we are becoming more like Christ, we're going to look different—maybe even a little crazy. Think about a glass of water. When you pour a little bit of salt into the water, the entire glass starts to taste salty. That's what the Lord does in our lives. Knowing the Lord should change everything, even our language. Jesus said that His followers were to be the salt of the earth—and that means our whole lives should be salty. We can't separate anything in our lives from our relationship with the Lord. We are His all the time, and He is committed to remaking us in the image of Jesus. We shouldn't be afraid to be different. The Lord uses His people to show a lost world something different—something better.

As I grew in my faith, I had to keep one thing in check: I had to remind myself that a moral life does not win favor with God. When the Lord changes us, we start to look different, and it's easy to think that we've done something good. We can even feel like God owes us something. But we could never be good enough to deserve God's love, and our morality will never impress Him. We are saved through faith in Christ alone. Our words and actions should flow out of a heart that has been changed by the Lord. We can't earn God's grace by doing good things. That wouldn't be grace. Grace means getting something that we really don't deserve. It's a relief to remember that God's grace doesn't depend on us or on our ability to live a perfect life. Thankfully, it depends on Jesus, who lived a perfect life for us and died in our place.

I used to panic when people asked me questions about my faith or "being different." I feared I wouldn't have the right answers. I've learned that what matters more is my attitude as I respond to questions. Sure, it helps to know the right answer, but a lot of times I really don't. I want to love people, and I want to be willing to talk about my faith. The Lord has helped me grow a lot in this area. It's all about how we respond to tough questions. Gently and with respect, I'm learning to communicate the hope that I have in Christ. From there, it is amazing where the Lord will lead a conversation.

It's awesome being in a baseball world where no two people look alike. Differences collide, and there are a lot of questions and opportunities to talk about the Lord. I tried to live differently in high school, but no one really challenged my faith with deep thoughts or tough questions. So it's good to pose a few questions for all of us to consider: Are we living in a way that causes others to ask why we look so different? Or are we doing everything we can just to blend in? When Christ is working in our lives, we can't help but change, and real change makes people raise their eyebrows and wonder why.

I wish that someone had challenged my faith in high school and asked me some hard questions. Even though my friends and I were different from the majority in some ways, it was still easy to blend in. Living for Christ is like swimming upstream, but I know now that it's worth it. The Minors were the beginning of a new chapter in my walk with the Lord. First He helped me to look different, and then He helped me to be okay with that. When people dare to be different, the Lord looks great in their lives. Is anyone asking you about the hope that you have? If your hope really is in Jesus, start praying for courage to live like that's true. Then, when the questions come, don't be afraid to talk about the One who makes you who you are. He wants you to look different. He wants you to look like Jesus—and the more you look like Jesus, the more people will be curious to know what makes you different.

# 16

## EVERY BEGINNING
## IS A STRUGGLE

Ellen

**The stories about me in kindergarten are notorious—and the trouble didn't end there.** I think I probably set the school record for having an emotional breakdown every year on the first day of school. While most kids in elementary school look forward to a new year, it was my greatest nightmare. I hated the thought of starting over in an unfamiliar classroom, with new friends, a new teacher and even a new lunch hour. "New" was terrifying to me because it thwarted my desperate attempt to keep everything the same. I embraced the familiar. Peanut butter and jelly for lunch every single day for 10 years was fine with me. I really didn't like it when things changed.

My parents tell stories of leaving me at school in a sobbing puddle. Thankfully, I had a string of loving teachers who welcomed me into their classrooms, tears and all. Looking back, I can see that change rocked my boat more than it did for others. I sometimes still recognize that same struggle in me today. However, I am encouraged by how much the Lord has challenged me to see the good in change. For a girl who took a "sick day" every time I had a substitute teacher, I have made dramatic progress. I now find it thrilling to jump on a plane to cross the Atlantic or move to California to begin life as a baseball wife. God has done something remarkable in my heart toward change.

Every beginning is a struggle. But a transition into something new can be really exciting. For instance, I loved buying matching bedding with my college roommate, getting that first stamp in my passport, and moving into a new apartment as a newlywed. Those have been really sweet parts of transition. However, I always have a slight hesitation that reminds me that I'm a work in progress. It's still hard saying goodbye to friends and family, knowing that a chapter of my life is complete. An even greater challenge is remembering who I am from one chapter of life to the next.

I think I can speak for most high school freshmen when I say that one of the greatest struggles of beginning at a new school is figuring out how to fit in. That was certainly the case for me, anyway. I wanted so much for people to like me and want to be my friend. I watched other people fighting the same battle and noticed how difficult it was for people who felt like they didn't fit in. Fortunately, I soon found my friends and the rhythm of being in a new world. By the time senior year rolled around, I was more comfortable in my own skin. Our group of friends had our weekend routine down. I never had to wonder whom I would sit with at lunch or at the baseball game. I had my friends, so the routine of high school fit me like a glove. After living in one community my whole life, I doubted that anything could be better. We still lived in the same house we had moved into when I was a baby. We even had our beloved dog, Ranger, who had been a part of the family since before I was born. Ranger was with us for 18 years. Things really didn't change too much—and I loved that.

I knew that college meant transition, but for some reason the thought was exciting to me. Even though I figured out pretty quickly that this new beginning had its own struggles, I also recognized its opportunities. Our graduating class scattered to universities all over the nation. If I ever had a chance to start over, this was it. I could go to college with a clean slate. If there was something I didn't like about myself, I could change it. I could redefine myself. I could make new friends, join a sorority, become a vegetarian—I could even change my name if I wanted to. No one would know the difference, because no one really knew me at college. There is great freedom in starting over, but with that freedom comes the danger that we'll forget who we are.

Clayton was learning the same lessons about transition in a totally different way. He entered the Minor Leagues at age 18, fresh out of high school. Clayton and I share similar stories in that Highland Park was really the only community that we knew. So after graduation, we both flew out of the nest, but in different directions—and we each had to fly alone. Clayton arrived in Vero Beach, Florida, with no familiar faces around him. Transition for him meant meeting new people from different places, with different backgrounds and beliefs. At least I had the comfort of staying in the same state with people who understood the word "y'all."

Learning to talk on the phone didn't come easily for us. Okay, fine—when I say "us," I mean Clayton. I could go off on a three-hour tangent without taking a breath. Clayton would sit on the other end, dumbfounded that I had so much to say. However, I do remember some amazing conversations when we stayed up late talking. I would sit outside of my college dorm, and he would sit outside the baseball dorm. We would talk each other through the new phase of life we were experiencing. We talked about the tension between wanting to belong and wanting to remain true to who we were. We talked about the struggle of transitioning and how fitting in can sometimes take precedence over being genuine. Thankfully, we could hold each other accountable. Even though friends back home knew that we were Christians, our new acquaintances didn't necessarily know that. We agreed that starting over was difficult, and yet there was a sense of freedom and excitement that came from new beginnings. For the first time, people looked at Clayton's actions and asked about his background and beliefs. Being associated with Christ sometimes made Clayton look odd to his teammates. In a different way, I understood that feeling. It was interesting figuring out how to express our faith when the people around us didn't always share it. Learning how to do that was a good challenge for both of us.

Clayton and I went to a high school where most people look and act the same. Most girls had long, straight hair, and most guys played a sport. Other high schools can be really different, but at our school it was completely accepted and even cool to be a Christian, or at least to claim to be a Christian. Most students chose just to fit in and go with the crowd. So when Clayton and I found ourselves in the melting pots of college and Minor League Baseball, our eyes were opened to the difference between an authentic Christian life and the rest of the world. We got our first taste of the "real world," you might say. Suddenly we weren't in a bubble where things felt comfortable and easy.

In every new beginning, I have to remember who I am in the Lord. Some parts of my identity have changed through the years. For instance, after high school graduation, I could no longer associate myself with the dance team. After college graduation, I could no longer identify myself with my sorority. However, my identity in Christ remains constant even as seasons change. Still, living out that identity can be a challenge, especially in unfamiliar environments. In college, I struggled to learn what it meant to have a genuine relationship with the Lord and not just say all the right things. In Africa, I learned that actions sometimes speak louder than words, especially when you don't speak the same language as the people around you. Of course words matter, but they don't mean much when our lives don't match our lips.

I started to think more about the Lord—who He is, and what He had done for me—and what that meant for my life. I realized that the Lord had been faithful to me for so many years, and I knew I couldn't find a secure identity anywhere but in Him. Clayton had to do the same thing. The Lord, who had helped us figure out who we were individually and together, continued to work on us as we focused on Him through our transitions. Many people drift away from the Lord after high school, and we easily could have taken the more comfortable route of blending in with the world that doesn't acknowledge God. Maintaining our faith challenged us at times, but the Lord convinced us that living for Him would be far more satisfying than living without Him.

The Lord uses new beginnings and transitions for His glory in our lives. He reminds me that, as much as everything seems to be changing, the most important things about me stay the same. Because of what Christ has done for me, I belong to Him. I am secure. Nothing can separate me from His love. Change tempts me to think that I have to redefine myself, but the Lord reminds me that I am defined by Him—and He never changes.

In the moment, transitions can be difficult and confusing; often it is only later that we can see how the Lord led us through the whole process. I remember being dropped off at my college dorm for the first time. It was a monumental moment, and I fought panic. But I knew the Lord was with me. His presence gave me peace. Then I remember going to Zambia for the first time. Based on past experiences, I should have been an emotional mess. Instead of feeling anxious, I found courage and strength in the Lord. I also saw the Lord's faithfulness as I waved goodbye to my family and drove off, bound for spring training as Clayton's wife. I could breathe a deep sigh of relief, knowing I was exactly where I should be.

The Lord has been so good to me—I'm not the same puddle of tears I was in kindergarten. God has brought me through a lot of new beginnings, and I've grown more confident that He will be with me through every transition. Right now, Clayton and I are right in the middle of another transition together—marriage. As we trace the Lord's goodness to us in the past, we joyfully look forward to what He will do in our marriage. Like other transitions, our latest adventure forces us to deal with the question "Who are you?" Once again, the Lord is using this season of change to remind us of all that we are in Christ.

Just because a transition is hard doesn't mean that the Lord isn't in control. My experience has taught me that even when everything feels out of control, He is graciously in control. When nothing makes sense, He is still there. When we feel empty, He fills us. When we are lost, He guides us. When life seems pointless, He is using the struggle for His purposes. We naturally resist change, but when everything is new in our lives, we can be confident that the Lord is doing something new in our lives, too. The Lord is with us through the struggles of every new beginning, and He is always good.

I like to picture my life as a tiny boat. A little rain comes, and this tiny boat starts getting wet and taking on water. But with each rain, the Lord works on this little boat and teaches me how to handle more water. I'm getting acclimated to the storms of life. By the grace of God, I'm learning how to float. Bigger rains demand more of my boat, but when they come, I know that He still controls the seas. The floods of transition don't have to terrify me. I see how the Lord has guided me through the storms of the past, and I know He will be with me through the next one. With each new chapter, He gives me an opportunity to sail through on the faith that looks to Him for everything I need. I can take on more water. I am a tiny boat, but I have a great Captain.

Clayton won the championship with his Little League team, the Dodgers.

Clayton and Ellen at homecoming during their sophomore year at Highland Park.

Clayton and Ellen during their first month of dating as freshmen in high school.

Clayton and Ellen after a high school baseball game.

Clayton threw a perfect game during the playoffs in high school, striking out 15 batters.

Clayton would play first base on his high school team in the games he did not pitch.

A team celebration at home plate after Clayton hit a home run.

Clayton and Ellen's families together for Christmas 2007.

Clayton and Ellen after their graduation from Highland Park High School in 2006.

Clayton and Ellen at the ranch.

Clayton with Ellen's family at their ranch in Texas.

Preston Mattingly and Clayton played for the Midland, Michigan Loons Single-A team during their first full season in the Minor Leagues.

Ellen on a visit to Jacksonville, Florida, where Clayton played for the Suns Double-A team.

In June 2006, Clayton was flown to Los Angeles for the first time to sign his Major League contract with the Dodgers. Here, he speaks with reporters at Dodger Stadium.

In 2008, Clayton was called up to the Major League spring training camp in Vero Beach, Florida.

Ellen with her siblings Jed, Ann and John.

Family and friends made the trip to Los Angeles to see Clayton's Major League debut on May 25, 2008.

Clayton and Ellen reunite outside the stadium after Clayton's first game with the Dodgers.

During Clayton's first off-season, he began a baseball clinic to raise funds for children in Africa.

Clayton got together with his high school buddies in Dallas during the Christmas break in 2008.

Clayton pitching at Dodger Stadium. In 2011 he led the league in wins (21), strikeouts (248) and earned run average (2.28), and he won the National League Cy Young Award.

Clayton, a left-handed strikeout pitcher, in 2011 won the Warren Spahn Award for best lefty.

Clayton and teammate Matt Kemp before a game in Dodger Stadium.

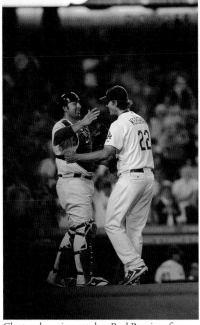

Clayton hugging catcher Rod Barajas after another complete game and win.

Clayton with his mom, Marianne.

Ellen surrounded by her college girlfriends at Texas A&M.

Close friends celebrate with the couple after Clayton proposed to Ellen in 2009.

Clayton and Ellen riding off after their wedding reception.

Clayton and Ellen walk the aisle after saying "I do" on December 4, 2010, in Dallas.

Ellen's first trip to Zambia in 2007, when she was 18 years old.

The children that Clayton and Ellen met during their first trip together to Zambia in 2010.

Clayton and Ellen with Hope, their inspiration for Kershaw's Challenge (above). In 2011, Clayton and Ellen gave $100 per batter he struck out during the season to build a new home for children like these in Zambia.

Clayton throws a ball down a dirt road in Zambia—keeping to his off-season workout routine.

Teaching kids how to play catch.

Showing this kid his baseball mitt.

# 17

# GROWING UP APART

Ellen

## Dear Clayton,

*You know, I've really come a long way. I started thinking the other day about the learning curve that I have experienced since we've been apart. I'm pretty proud of myself. Here are a few things that I wanted to point out.*

*Things I have learned in 2007:*

1. *I've learned that we should never have a serious conversation after midnight. We're both exhausted and nothing makes sense.*
2. *I've learned that baseball is a game with 9 innings and 9 players on the field at a time. After years of watching my brothers and you play baseball, I am finally paying attention.*
3. *I've learned that the Red Sox are in Boston.*
4. *I've learned that doing homework by myself and for myself is not fun. I'm also not very good at studying without you there to make me.*
5. *I've learned that air hockey is not something to be taken lightly.*
6. *I've learned the proper way to throw a fastball—thanks to my pitching coach and pink baseball glove.*
7. *I've learned that cheering, "Go, Clayton!" at a baseball game can be a piercing shrill that gets a rise out of the entire section.*
8. *I've learned that my car doesn't run on diesel. They say the diesel nozzle won't fit in a regular car. I can prove them wrong.*
9. *I've learned that phone calls from you have become just as great as seeing you in person.*
10. *I've learned that you truly don't know what you've got 'til it's gone.*

*So here we are. You're in Florida and I'm here in College Station, and we're making it work, one day at a time . . . until we see each other again.*

*Love, Ellen*

Yeah, I was "that" girl in college. I came to school with a long-distance boyfriend who didn't even live in the same state. Emails, like the one above, became one of the primary ways we stayed in touch. I showed up as a freshman at Texas A&M University excited to jump in. I went through rush week and ended up joining a sorority, which turned out to be a tremendous blessing in my life. I was immediately part of a community. It was nice to be walking through this new season with 50 other freshman girls. We were from all over the place, but I quickly learned how much we had in common. I found my best friends in college. But none of them knew anything about this boy who was hundreds of miles away.

I remember the first date party we had during the fall of my freshman year—"Bingo and Barbecue." All of my pledge sisters were busy finding dates and setting up other people with blind dates for the party. For the first time, I had to think about going to a party without Clayton. In high school, we went to everything together—homecoming, prom, baseball banquets. He was my "go-to" and the only guy I had been with in a date situation. Because I had to take a date to our sorority functions, I quickly developed my qualified invitation speech. I would invite someone to come with me as my date, as long as he was fully aware that Clayton was in the picture. Thankfully, I had so many high school friends with me at Texas A&M that it wasn't a problem. But it was a change for me. That year marked the beginning of us growing up apart from each other.

Ultimately, the years that we spent in two different states were great for us. From ages 14 to 18, we had done everything together, including holidays with our families. Senior year of high school was truly charmed. We spent that year with a great group of friends. Starting over after graduation was a little like having the rug pulled out from under us. Clayton and I were back to square one—meeting new people, making first impressions, and wishing that we could be together.

Suddenly we found ourselves in two different worlds that didn't have much in common. Our schedules were completely opposite. I went to class during the day, but I had time to talk at night. Clayton had more freedom during the day, but he had games at night. We were totally missing each other. So we had two options. We could either throw in the towel and call it quits, or we could get creative. A relationship is much easier when you live eight blocks from each other and have the same class schedule. Our first year apart was trying because it was so different from anything we had known before. But we battled through it and came to the conclusion that our relationship was worth the fight.

Being so far apart forced us to grow up apart, and that turned out to be a good thing. Our circumstances pushed us toward greater dependence on the Lord. It's easy to depend on and confide in another person when that person is right next to you all the time—and that makes it hard to learn to take your needs to the Lord first. The hidden blessing in being miles apart was that we found the Lord to be more consistent than the other person. I began to meet with the Lord when I couldn't get in touch with Clayton. I prayed more because I wasn't able to talk to Clayton whenever I wanted. We both realized that in some ways, the comfort of growing up together had stunted our growth in the Lord. Time apart gave us room to reestablish our identities in Christ first. It was hard to detach and figure things out on my own. But it was also a huge blessing.

A personal relationship with Jesus is unlike any other relationship we will ever have. Sometimes when we grow up in a strong community of believers, we can struggle to take ownership of our faith. When Clayton and I graduated from high school, starting over was hard. But it drove us to the Lord. Those years were really important for me. Christ became more satisfying to me than any other relationship, even my relationship with Clayton. I could tell that Clayton was learning the same thing. Years later, when we started talking about marriage, loving the Lord first—the lesson we had learned while growing up apart—became the foundation of our new chapter together.

The most shocking part of our time apart was that I had to figure out how to do my own homework. Clayton and I had always done it together. I confess that sometimes he even finished mine when I ran out of time. In a very practical way, I had to figure out how to stay afloat on my own. College studies were different from high school assignments. Not having Clayton around to bail me out really held my feet to the fire. But even that was good for me. I had to learn how to make life work without someone by my side all of the time. College gave me so much more than a diploma. Those years gave me a chance to grow up in ways that I really needed to.

So it took us a few months, but we eventually figured out our routine. Phone conversations happened at odd times of the day and night, and usually only lasted a few minutes. But we did what we had to do to make things work. Clayton told me about his new friends that I had never met; I told him about a group of girls who were loving and encouraging in a way that I had never known. Each of us was excited for the other, but we were also excited to get back to being face to face.

During my freshman year and Clayton's first season, we only saw each other once. I met him in Los Angeles for the ESPY Awards. Clayton had been nominated as a Gatorade High School Player of the Year, and his mom and I went along as guests. We had been apart for several months. But when I saw him for the first time wearing a suit and signing autographs in the hotel lobby, I felt like he had already aged 10 years. We had both survived the first couple of months out on our own. We had taken steps toward maturity in our vastly different worlds. Those few days in L.A. flew by. We barely had time to catch up before I was back on a plane to Texas. We both realized how important it was to ask the Lord to keep our hearts aligned, because our lives seemed to be heading in completely different directions. I returned to school with great stories of meeting famous, professional athletes—most of whom I had never even heard of. That was my first taste of California. The girls back in College Station soon figured out that this boy was more than just a high school flame. He was my best friend, and I couldn't wait for them to meet him.

Once the season ended, Clayton made the drive to visit me at school. He would spend the next four off-seasons traveling back and forth between Dallas and College Station. He got his taste of the college experience as he crashed on various friends' couches. We always had a few date parties late in the fall that Clayton was able to attend with me. My friends got to know him, and I got to see my two worlds finally come together. Clayton and I were known for coming up with epic costumes for the themed parties. Our repertoire included turkeys, yodelers, and the Griswold couple from Chevy Chase's *Christmas Vacation*. Clayton and I tore it up on the dance floor, and he got to know all of my new best friends. People would ask him where he went to school, and he would simply answer, "Oh, I don't go to school." Come on! Give them something—make up anything! It sounded like I was dating a high school drop-out. But he was perfectly fine with leaving it that simple. Even though our new homes were far apart, there were moments that made us feel like we were living the same life together. I'm grateful for our two worlds and how quickly they became one.

Moving away from your best friend is never easy. Parts of the process were really tough, but I learned to see all the things that made the separation worthwhile. We had to get good at talking on the phone and retelling stories from the day. We learned the importance of asking good questions so we could continue to get to know each other. Sometimes it felt like we lived from visit to visit. But God gave us grace to realize early on that our time apart was important. Our two worlds gave us different experiences that enriched our relationship. It was a really sweet thing to grow up together in the same neighborhood, but the Lord was also gracious to give us time apart. We realized our need for Him and began to appreciate life even when our best friend seemed worlds away.

# 18

## THE MOST RIDICULOUS FEELING IN THE WORLD

Clayton

**I never would have seen Zebulon, North Carolina, if it weren't for baseball.** The Minor Leagues take you all over the country to places you've never heard of before. There's something special about these little towns with a big love for baseball. You find people who welcome you with open arms because they love the game as much as you do. Baseball is the universal language from places like Zebulon, North Carolina, to Midland, Michigan, where I played for the Great Lakes Loons. When I was playing for the Jacksonville Suns, the Carolina Mudcats were one of our fiercest rivals. Zebulon happens to be home to the Mudcats, so that's where we were headed in May 2008. We took a 12-hour bus trip through the middle of the night from Jacksonville, Florida. Stiff from the bus ride, we arrived at the hotel in time to get a decent meal and then crash—our normal routine for road trips. I was scheduled to pitch the next day.

We arrived at the field in plenty of time to go about our normal preparations, like playing cards and throwing long toss across the field. The game started, and soon it came time for me to take the mound against our rivals. I made it through the first inning with ease. Coming back to the dugout, I sat down and waited to go in again. I was surprised when the manager looked at me and, without hesitation, said, "You're done." I panicked, thinking I had done something to deserve getting pulled from the game. There was always a mind game of thinking that you might get sent back down to a lower level in the Minors.

"What are you talking about?" I asked, slightly unnerved. "It's just the first inning! And I'm not doing bad yet!"

The manager maintained his composure and calmly replied, "Trust me. You're done. I can't tell you why, but you're definitely done." My heart sank as I slumped back against the bench. What could possibly be going on? I thought my game had been on target, so the thought of getting demoted felt defeating.

All of a sudden, rumors began flying around the dugout, as people tried to make sense of my brief outing. It was hard not to notice the starting pitcher still sitting on the bench as a new pitcher warmed up. I went back to the clubhouse to ice my arm that had been fully warmed up and then pulled from the game. I felt nervous, having no idea what was going on. The coaches kept their cool, as if watching me squirm was the afternoon's entertainment. Sure enough, they made me wait through the entire eight remaining innings, offering me nothing to contradict the assumption that I had screwed up.

After the game, we all retreated into the clubhouse to shower and eat. It was business as usual. Everyone else followed the normal routine, so I did the same thing. Then the manager hollered across the room for me to step into his office. This was it. At least I knew it was coming. I figured I would be leaving for another minor league team that day. I walked in, and he handed me the phone. "Clayton, it's for you. Ned Colletti wants to talk to you." Ned Colletti is the General Manager of the Los Angeles Dodgers. *Man*, I thought, *I really screwed this one up*. Wanting to make a good impression, I tried to collect myself as I took the phone.

Mr. Colletti didn't waste any time. "Clayton, you are coming up. You're pitching this Sunday here in Los Angeles. You will be catching the first flight out on Saturday. We're excited to see you then."

That was it. I was moving to another team, but in the completely opposite direction than I had expected. I had just received my call to the Big Leagues. That was the most unreal feeling in the world. Mr. Colletti told me to keep things quiet until the shifts within the team were final. When one player moves up, someone else moves down. That reality is never easy to swallow, but it's the business of baseball. So I had to play it cool, walking back into the clubhouse and grabbing my things like nothing had happened. Once outside, I called Ellen. She was in a room full of our friends, who were home for the summer. I told her not to say anything, but to find a flight to L.A. as soon as possible. I had been moved up. This was my big shot to play in Dodger Stadium, and I wanted her to be there with me.

The bag I had packed for the Zebulon road trip included a pair of shorts and old T-shirts. That's it. I owned a suit, but it was back in Jacksonville with the rest of my belongings. It's not hard to pack when you don't have any options. I asked Ellen to raid my closet at home in Dallas and grab anything nice she could find. I figured shorts and a T-shirt might be a little too casual for the Big Leagues.

The flight on Saturday took off from Zebulon and headed west. After riding on a bus all over the Southeast, taking an airplane to Los Angeles was huge. An airplane meant that something big had just happened. By the next day, people started hearing the news. My teammates were so encouraging and supportive. It was humbling to receive the call that we all work so hard to receive. My mom and Ellen quietly rallied the troops in Dallas. My best friends, Mom, Ellen and her family jumped on a plane to meet me in L.A.

Disheveled but excited, I boarded the plane first thing Saturday morning. In preparation for arriving in L.A., I checked the Dodgers' schedule to see who our opponent would be. We were in the middle of a series with the St. Louis Cardinals. That meant I would be facing some tough hitters such as Troy Glaus, who had led the Angels to the World Series championship a few years earlier—and I would face a hero of mine, Albert Pujols, who has been hitting home runs for the Cardinals since I started high school! It was a surreal moment. My dream was unfolding before my eyes.

Zebulon, North Carolina, might just be a dot on the map for most people, but for me, it will always be a significant place. That's where I received the call—and it really was the most ridiculous feeling I have ever experienced. The Lord has been gracious to me during this crazy journey. He never ceases to amaze me. I stepped off the plane at the Los Angeles International Airport. I wasn't there for a West Coast vacation. I was there to play baseball for the Los Angeles Dodgers. I blended into the busy terminal, carrying everything I had with me in a small duffel bag. There was a pit in my stomach as I realized the weightiness of this moment. It was comforting to know that my family was on the way. The shock of the call to come to the Big Leagues made for an interesting few days. I guess most people don't travel to Zebulon, North Carolina, thinking that a once-in-a-lifetime moment is about to come their way.

# 19

# WELCOME TO
# THE MAJOR LEAGUES

Clayton

**My heart was thumping so loudly I could barely hear the National Anthem ringing through Dodger Stadium.** It was like a kick drum keeping a steady beat, and I was convinced that everyone around me could hear its boom. My hands were sweaty, and I was sure that if I tried to take a deep breath, I'd lose my cool and burst into a smile. That would not have been cool. I had to pull myself together. Even though this was my first time standing in a Dodger uniform as part of the team, I had to act like I belonged. Showing any emotion would blow my cover. "No big deal, this is just another game." Yeah, right. Maybe people wouldn't notice the new kid on the sidelines. The National Anthem reverberated through the stadium, and I felt like I was hearing it for the first time. It sounded incredible. Suddenly, something caught my eye. I looked up at the big screen—where I saw something that made my heart skip two beats and then drop into my stomach. I wished in that moment that the field would open up and swallow me whole.

That was my "welcome to the Major Leagues" moment. Thankfully, I can now look back and laugh about it. But at the time, I wanted to crawl into a hole and disappear. Two days earlier, I had received the phone call of a lifetime from Ned Colletti, the Dodgers general manager. I was scheduled to be the starting pitcher in L.A. on Sunday. I arrived at the Los Angeles International Airport on Saturday morning. My head was spinning. I was picked up and taken directly to Dodger Stadium. The travel time on my flight and in the car gave me a chance to think about things. This was a big moment and I knew it. I also knew that I couldn't possibly take it all in. Ellen and our families would be arriving later that day to share in the excitement. That gave me confidence. I set my sights on Sunday: my first Major League game.

As we drove through Los Angeles, I could hardly believe my eyes. Could this really be happening? Riding up toward Dodger Stadium, I noticed that the parking lots were already full. People in blue and white streamed into the stadium to watch the game. I felt like one of them—a star-struck fan with a chance to see a game at this legendary ballpark. To my surprise, the car dropped me off at the players' entrance, a jolting reminder that I wasn't just a spectator. I was there to play. I grabbed my one duffel bag with all of my belongings and stood in the shadow of a stadium worn with time and surrounded by palm trees. Dodger Stadium.

I was escorted to the player clubhouse, where I was determined to keep my composure. My jaw dropped as I looked around. I had never seen anything like it. It was so organized and clean—nothing like the locker rooms from high school and the Minors. I walked past the individual lockers, quietly looking at every name above the cubbies. These were the guys I had been watching. They were living the life I had dreamed about living. Now they were my teammates. The guy showing me around stopped in front of one locker in particular, and I noticed the name at the top—Kershaw. Even though I was so new to the team, I suddenly felt a part of it. They knew I was coming. Seeing my own name had never been so surreal.

Most of the guys were already on the field, warming up. I was instructed to change into a uniform and join them in time for the game. The guys who were still in the clubhouse really made me feel welcome. They came up, introduced themselves and said they were excited to play together. I've never been great at multitasking, and the events of the following moments prove my point. Someone was talking to me, and I was trying to engage in the conversation while also getting ready for the game. Leaning back in my chair, I reached for the jersey that was hanging behind me. By the way, the jersey also had my name on it. That was pretty cool as well. I wasn't just a number. I was a number and a name. I had dreamed of this day.

I wasn't paying too much attention to what I was doing. Unknowingly, I reached into the locker next to mine and pulled out Jason Schmidt's jersey. Caught up in talking and nervousness, I didn't notice the mistake as I pulled Jason's jersey on and tucked it in. Jason was standing nearby and watched the scene unfold. Recognizing the opportunity to make my first game a memorable one, he casually reached into my locker (again, without me noticing) and put on my jersey. Everything looked good to me! He had on a Dodger jersey, and so did I. Game time.

The unbelievable moments continued to pile up, one after another. Jason and I walked into the dugout, just minutes before game time. I stood shoulder-to-shoulder with guys who were living legends to me. Joe Torre came over to shake my hand and welcome me to the Big Leagues. I knew that being under his coaching would be an experience of a lifetime. I have never seen Dodger Stadium look as spectacular as it did on that day.

The players were called to the field for the National Anthem. I figured I didn't need to go because I wasn't playing that day. But Jason elbowed me to come, so I jumped to my feet. Once we were standing on the field, Jason pointed to a spot. "You need to stand here for the National Anthem," he said. That sounded a little weird to me, but I wasn't about to ask questions. "Don't worry," Jason said, "I'll stand right behind you so that you don't feel awkward."

The anthem started—and that's when it happened. At first, I was caught up in the moment, but then suddenly I noticed the camera circling back around toward me. *This must be normal*, I thought. The guy with the camera came around behind me and got a close-up of my back. That seemed strange enough that I glanced up at the big screen to see what was going on. The guys behind me started cracking up, and after a few moments (which felt like 20 minutes), I realized what was so funny. The camera shot showed the back of my jersey. Only it wasn't *my* jersey. "Schmidt, 29" is what the uniform said. Schmidt—not Kershaw. The cameraman, in on the joke, whipped around and captured Jason, who was standing right behind me, enjoying this hysterical and bizarre moment at my expense—and in *my* jersey.

The stadium erupted in laughter . . . during the National Anthem . . . at me. My face dropped, though I couldn't help but laugh. *Way to make an entrance, Clayton*, I thought. The anthem must have lasted longer than it ever had before. I lost track of time as I tried to calculate how long I had to stand on the field in the wrong jersey. At last, the song ended, and we all piled back into the dugout. Jason took off my jersey, and I finally got to put it on. My own Dodger jersey.

For the most part, we prefer to forget embarrassing moments. We wish they had never happened. But as embarrassing as that moment was for me, I'll never regret it. It was my "welcome to the Major Leagues" moment. When Ellen and our families arrived that evening, I was reluctant to tell them the story. But I knew they would hear it from someone else if they didn't hear it from me. At least if I told them, I could try to defend myself. I will never forget that first game. Even if I could, my teammates would be sure to remind me. I can't remember who sang the National Anthem that day. I just remember that it was the longest, most grueling, and most memorable version I have ever heard at a baseball game.

# 20

# "MAN, PUJOLS IS GOOD"

## Clayton

**You know that feeling when you've got so much on your mind that you can't sleep?** You lie awake, just staring at the ceiling. Sometimes you have great breakthrough ideas, but most of the time your thoughts just multiply, and whatever you're worried about seems like a bigger deal than it really is. Then there are those times when you can't sleep because the next day holds something really important. You can't drift off because you're excited or nervous or a mixture of both. The night before my first Major League start felt just like that. I had been waiting my entire life for that day, and now, suddenly, it was here. Only a single night's sleep stood between me and one of the biggest days of my life. I really tried to get some good sleep that night. But when the lights went out and my body slowed down, my mind continued to race. It's maddening when you know you need to sleep, but you just can't.

Earlier that day, Ellen and our families had arrived in Los Angeles. I had flown in from Zebulon, North Carolina, a few hours before that. I could hardly believe it was my turn to have a shot at the Majors, and I was relieved to have familiar faces there with me. My buddies from home came in as well, bringing comic relief with them. That night we hung out around the hotel. I called it an early night to make sure I got enough sleep. Then I sat up in bed, waiting for signs that I might be getting tired. Ellen and I talked on the phone, a routine we had started years before. She was a few rooms away, but she could tell how nervous I was. An opportunity to debut in the Major Leagues doesn't come along every day. Ellen is the perfect fit for me because she can read me like a book, even when I can't express how I'm feeling. My heart rate slowed as she reminded me of God's goodness and His control over the game. I knew God was in control—but it was also easy to forget. I suppose I got a few hours of sleep that night, but it hardly seemed like it.

I watched every hour tick across the fluorescent hotel clock on the bedside table.

By the grace of God, when morning rolled around, I actually felt refreshed. It was game day. I had to be at the field in the morning, because the game was scheduled for early afternoon. So I got up and took off for Dodger Stadium. The next few hours were a total blur. I was so distracted by the thought of throwing the first pitch that I hardly remember the hours leading up to that moment. I sat in the clubhouse, waiting to be called to the field to warm up. The minutes felt like hours. I thought that game time would never come. I made sure I was wearing my own jersey this time. But then all I could do was wait. Finally, I got the call to head to the field.

I knew my friends and family were in the stadium, but I was too distracted to pay attention to where they were sitting. I later found out that they had been sitting right in my line of sight from the mound. Apparently, they made quite a scene that day. Thankfully, I wasn't aware of anything other than doing my job. As I sat in the dugout, waiting for the game to begin, it felt like my heart was beating out of my chest. All I could think about was getting that first pitch over the plate. I leaned my head back against the dugout wall and took a deep breath. I knew I needed help. Closing my eyes, I asked the Lord for perspective: "Lord, whatever happens, be with me. Be my strength today." Since that day, I've prayed that same prayer before every game. I know that apart from the Lord, I have nothing to give. Not even a great first pitch. The Lord is my strength and the Giver of all good gifts. I had to remind myself of those truths that day and every day since.

I thought about the weight of the game before me. I felt like a kid who had just stepped into a man's world. My dream had come true. I hoped that it would be a great game, but I had played baseball long enough to realize that it could just as easily be a really rough game. Either way, I couldn't let it consume me. It was a big deal—but it was also just a game. I had to keep telling myself that. Winning this game would be awesome, but it wouldn't ultimately satisfy me. That's the way it goes with things in this world. There is a lot of good stuff to enjoy, but the things of the world will wear out and leave us wanting more. We can't find true satisfaction in them. But with God, we can be completely satisfied, knowing that He is everything.

I put my head down and focused on the task ahead. As if there wasn't enough pressure, we were playing the St. Louis Cardinals. So much for easing my way into the Majors! The time finally came. I took the mound and zeroed in on the catcher, Russell Martin. I threw a few practice pitches and tried to block out the sights and sounds around me. I had to stay focused. But it was hard to ignore the fact that I was standing on the mound in Dodger Stadium. Ridiculous.

The first batter stepped up to the plate. I threw the first pitch and instantly relaxed. It was really a wild moment. It was like my entire body exhaled as the pitch crossed the plate. To my relief, I struck that first batter out. Russell held onto the ball and tossed it toward the dugout. I panicked and trotted toward him. "What's the deal? Can I have the ball back?"

He laughed and said, "Relax, here's a new one." They were saving that first ball for me to keep. I still have it sitting on my desk back at home.

The second batter gave me a little more trouble. I ended up putting him on first base with a walk. The third batter was one I had been anticipating—Albert Pujols. He was and still is arguably the best hitter in the game. Not to mention he was a childhood hero of mine. I tried to block out the fact that it was Pujols standing at the plate. I just did my best to go after him. Before long, I had him sitting there with a full count—three balls and two strikes. This next pitch mattered. Russell called for a curveball and I thought, *If I throw this for a strike, there's no way he'd be expecting it.* Yeah, right. He hit the ball for a double and brought in a run. It was my first inning, and we were already losing. I circled the mound, trying to regain my composure for the next batter. I laughed to myself. This was insane. Albert Pujols was perched on second base behind me. I knew I needed to focus on the batter ahead of me. I had just given up a hit and a run. But still, it was quite an "I guess I'm in the Big Leagues" moment. It felt pretty cool.

I had the time of my life that day. I threw six innings, and we ended up winning the game 4-3 on a walk-off single by Andre Ethier in the bottom of the tenth. After the game, I went down into the clubhouse to shower and change. I had told Ellen to meet me with the rest of the group from home at the players' parking lot. I walked out into the lot and saw everyone. It was awesome to know that they had experienced the whole day with me. My buddies all gathered around, and one of them asked, "So, how was it?"

So many different thoughts raced through my mind, but only one came to the surface. I shook my head and said, "Man, Pujols is GOOD." I had always known that. But that day, I saw it first hand.

The team was boarding the buses behind me. We were heading to the airport for my first Big League road trip. The game I had been waiting for my whole life had gone as quickly as it came. I hugged everyone goodbye, thanking them for making the trip. As I sat on the bus on the way to the airport, the reality of the moment sank in. I had just played my first Major League game—against the St. Louis Cardinals and Albert Pujols. I would go up against them again in the future, but nothing would ever compare to that first face-off. The picture of Pujols staring me down from home plate will be etched in my mind forever.

Big moments in life are often hard to describe. We can't fully grasp everything that's happening, much less put it all into words. That day was one of those moments. As much as I tried to take it all in, it was just more than I could comprehend. When the Lord does something big in our lives, sometimes it's best just to sit back and soak it up. It frees us up to enjoy it more when we realize that we'll never be able to make sense of it all. That's how I felt that day. I can't remember every detail of the game, but some are crystal clear. I'll remember them—as well as the day as a whole—for the rest of my life. I didn't want to give up that one hit in the first inning. But if it had to happen, I'm happy to say I gave up my first Major League hit to Albert Pujols.

# 21

## HE MUST BECOME GREATER;
## I MUST BECOME LESS

Clayton

**I had just finished my first Major League season.** Nothing beats getting to play baseball for a living, but there is also something really great about coming home for the off-season. Dallas will always be home for me. That's where my mom and friends are, and after my first season, that's where Ellen was. We had gotten used to the long-distance dating thing. Knowing that we both would be in the same city for a month over the holidays kept us going.

Ellen and I had decided to host a baseball camp at the high school field after Christmas that year. Our goal was to raise support for the work Ellen had started in Africa several years back. We thought that a baseball day camp would be a great way to combine our two passions of baseball and mission work. Parents started registering their sons for the camp, and it seemed as though we would have a great turnout. The new varsity coach at Highland Park supported what we were doing, and the high school players were excited to help with the camp.

The day of the camp finally arrived, and we were all set. I had stations marked out across the field for kids to practice base running, hitting, pitching, and catching fly balls. As the kids rolled in that morning, I noticed the number of campers wearing my jersey. Some came in their Little League uniforms, but others came decked out in Dodger blue hats and shirts. Seeing my name across the backs of so many shirts startled me. Growing up, I had gone to baseball camps myself. I would look at the guys teaching the camp, and I wanted to be just like them. I probably came wearing the jersey of my favorite player, too. In that moment, watching kids race around the field in jerseys representing different teams and players, it struck me that I was now on the other side of the player-fan relationship. That thought humbled me. My dream had become reality, and I was actually living it. I wanted to make the most of the opportunity.

At the end of the day, I gathered all of the kids and had a chance to offer some encouragement and take some questions. A few hands shot up with questions about baseball, playing in the Major Leagues, and what it was like playing against baseball greats like Andy Pettitte. I laughed to myself because I knew I would have asked the same questions at their age. As camp was wrapping up, I sat down in the dugout and, to my surprise, saw a line of boys forming in front of me. They wanted autographs and pictures. That was an awesome moment for me. As I signed the kids' hats, balls, baseball cards and whatever else, I remembered what it was like to be their age. There was nothing cooler to me than playing baseball and getting autographs from players. Signing an autograph isn't a big deal to me now, but I remember what an autograph meant to me when I was a kid.

Playing baseball has been one of my greatest joys. But it has also been one of the most challenging experiences of my life. Professional sports hold an interesting place in our culture. People give athletes a lot of credit that they probably don't deserve. I play baseball because I love it, but I recognize that knowing how to throw a ball isn't an ability I developed on my own. It's a gift from the Lord. I've never been someone who longs for the spotlight. In fact, it always makes me feel pretty awkward. Just ask Ellen. It helps to remember that the Lord has given me this platform to make Him look great. What John the Baptist says about Jesus in John 3:30 is a great reminder to me: "He must become greater; I must become less." Anything that I have to offer is worthless if Christ is not moving in and through it. So in all that I do, God is glorified the most when His name stands out and my name shrinks.

We all have different spheres of influence. Mine happens to be playing baseball. Wherever you find yourself, you have a sphere of influence and a chance to use your life and gifts for something great. It doesn't matter how big or small your platform is. You could be a leader at school or among your friends. You could have an opportunity in an extracurricular activity or on a team. You could even have a platform in your family. Wherever we are, the

Lord wants to use us right there. We don't have to accomplish something great in the world's eyes to make Christ look great. Each of us has an important purpose from the Lord. As we live in Him, I believe He wants to shine through our lives. He must become greater; we must become less. Many people may never read a Bible, but they can learn about Christ as they watch the life of someone who makes Him look great. At the end of my career, I hope that people see Jesus more than they see me.

Jesus Christ gives us the ultimate example of how to live for and glorify God. When I look at the life of Christ, I see that it is marked with great humility and a high awareness of others. The humility of Christ is overwhelming to me when I consider who He really is. In his letter to the Philippians, the apostle Paul paints an incredible picture:

> If you have any encouragement from being united with Christ, if any comfort from his love, if any fellowship with the Spirit, if any tenderness and compassion, then make my joy complete by being like-minded, having the same love, being one in spirit and purpose. Do nothing out of selfish ambition or vain conceit, but in humility consider others better than yourselves. Each of you should look not only to your own interests, but also to the interests of the others. Your attitude should be the same as that of Christ Jesus:
>
> Who, being in very nature God, did not consider equality with God something to be grasped, but made himself nothing, taking the very nature of a servant, being made in human likeness. And being found in appearance as a man, he humbled himself and became obedient to death—even death on a cross! Therefore God exalted him to the highest place and gave him the name that is above every name, that at the name of Jesus every knee should bow, in heaven and on earth and under the earth, and every tongue confess that Jesus Christ is Lord, to the glory of God the Father (Phil. 2:1-11).

Christ's example of humility holds us to a new standard of considering others better than ourselves. As believers, we should grow to look more and more like Jesus. Paul says that in our relationships, we should have the same mindset as Christ, who put others before Himself. Ellen and I have had incredible opportunities to practice this mindset in Africa as we seek out ways to serve people there. But you don't have to go halfway around the world to serve as Christ did. You can do that right where you are. You can pray, "He must become greater; I must become less." You can ask the Lord to show you all the opportunities you have in your daily life to make an impact. The Lord can change our hearts and our attitudes so that we really do want Him to get the glory. Christ-like humility is a beautiful thing.

The Lord uses a lot of things to keep me humble. Remembering what Jesus did for me is the biggest thing. It's incredibly humbling to consider how Christ lived and died and rose for me. The trials that the Lord sends into our lives keep us humble, too. I think that's one of God's main purposes in our trials. If everything went perfectly in our lives, we wouldn't feel a need for Christ. He graciously brings things into my life that remind me how much I need Him. He humbles me and continues to become greater in my life. As if all this wasn't enough, it's helpful to have friends who have known me for my entire life! They remember when I was short, chubby, and even more awkward than I am today. They're always standing by with stories and memories that keep me levelheaded.

When I think about humility, I want to think about Jesus. I don't want to think about trying to act a certain way or be something that I'm not. I just want Him to become greater as I become less. I want the Lord to affect me in every area of my life—from marriage to the baseball field, from Africa to the way I interact with others. Jesus calls us to a different way of thinking about others and even about ourselves. He lived with a passion for God's glory and a longing to bring others to Him. With His help, I hope to do the same thing. It is not an easy task with worldly temptations around us, and we will continually fail because of the sin in our lives. But that should never stop us from running toward the Lord. With every game and every day of my life, He must become greater.

# 22

## The Mercy of Remembering You're Not Everything

Clayton

**Do you remember that feeling of getting in trouble when you were little?** What about the pit in your stomach when you got called into the principal's office? You knew you had done something wrong. You knew you didn't live up to expectations. Then, as if you weren't already aware of your mistake, someone else had to tell you about it. You sat down in front of a big desk and braced yourself for what was coming.

It can be hard to outgrow those feelings. No matter how old we get, we still have this desire to please people. As a result, it's tough to hear criticism. When I arrived in Los Angeles, I knew that the bar was set pretty high. I was only 21 years old, and I was playing against living legends. But still the expectations were high. I knew that my performance mattered. If I didn't hold up my end of the deal, someone would call me out.

It was early in the 2009 baseball season. I had just made my Major League debut the year before, so everything was still new to me. Making it to the Major Leagues is really hard; staying there is even harder. A few bad pitches and you can be sent right back down to the Minors. As much as I wanted to focus on the job at hand, I always had this fear in the back of my mind that I could get sent back down.

My season had gotten off to a rough start, and sure enough, the manager called me into his office. That elementary school pit in my stomach was back again. Except this was about more than getting in trouble. This was about my career and my dream. The manager was straightforward with me. We talked about how things were going, and I agreed with him that I wasn't off to a great start. After a long conversation about my shortcomings, his expectations, and ways I could improve, I promised the skipper that I would continue to work hard and focus on the results that were expected of me. To be given the opportunity to stay in the Majors and work on my game was a huge relief. But feeling like I wasn't measuring up was painful and humbling.

It's tough when someone tells you that you're not performing well. I wanted so much to fix it. I wanted to work harder and put in longer hours. I was desperate to do whatever it would take to improve. My conversation with the manager at the beginning of the 2009 season got me thinking about the relationship between faith and performance. Whenever our performance doesn't measure up, it's easy to start wondering if people will think about us the same way—and then we apply those thoughts to our relationship with God. But God doesn't base His love for us on our performance—and if we accept that truth, we will find freedom from the fear of failure. There is nothing we can do to make the Lord love us more, and there is nothing we can do to make the Lord love us less. His love for us is consistent. No matter what I do, or what I fail to do, the Lord doesn't change. That's what I needed to remember when the manager wanted more, and that's what I need to remember every day in my walk with Jesus.

It's incredibly comforting to know that when I pitch a terrible game, the Lord is still with me. Because of Jesus, I still have my salvation. That is untouchable. God loves me because that is who He is, not because I deserve it. Somehow we have wrongly convinced ourselves that God's love depends on our performance. In reality, what we accomplish or leave unfinished can't change who He is and how He has decided to relate to His people. No matter how well or poorly we perform at any given task (in my case, whether I pitch a shut-out or give up half a dozen home runs), our worth is secure in the Lord. Until we figure this out, we'll never really have peace and joy. We'll always fear getting the rug pulled out from under us whenever we fall short. And we all fall short!

Trials and failures do not define us. They build steel into the foundation of our lives and help us become the people the Lord wants us to be. So I don't regret those tough times that humble me and drive me to my knees, because they convict me to listen to His call and seek His will. I know that I am not defined by performance or achievements. Bad pitches and losses simply remind me that I'm not perfect. We all need moments like that so we can know the mercy of His unequaled love. He is, after all, the ultimate Coach.

Ellen and I have learned a lot about this mercy in Africa. Out of my comfort zone and fully overwhelmed by the needs of Zambian orphans, I was struck by the reality that we could not be everything to these children. As we walked through the impoverished villages, I understood why Ellen's heart ached to adopt every child in sight. I wanted to do the same thing. Though God ordains and allows hard times to conform us to the image of Christ, how could we desire to do anything less than change the world for these kids? We're excited to continue doing ministry in Africa, because we see the Lord at work in big ways. But it's tough to remember that we can't save the children we meet. We can't change their hearts. What we can do is point them to the One who offers them something better—Jesus. It's overwhelming to see the need and pain in Africa. We wish we could do more, but we're not in control. The Lord is in control, though, and He knows every heart and every life. It is easier to come home to America knowing that the Lord stays with those kids in Africa.

God is merciful to remind us that we're not everything. In baseball, I won't always play my best game. But that doesn't change how the Lord sees me. I can deal with a bad game. I can also trust the Lord when I hear a heartbreaking story from an African child. The Lord uses what's tough to keep me dependent on Him. In the Bible, the book of James talks about going through trials. One passage has been particularly encouraging to me when I think about going through hard times:

> Consider it pure joy, my brothers, whenever you face trials of many kinds, because you know that the testing of your faith develops perseverance. Perseverance must finish its work so that you may be mature and complete, not lacking anything (Jas. 1:2-4).

It's a little strange to be joyful about a trial. How is that even possible? I think James wants us to realize that we can be joyful in a trial because God uses trials to grow us up in our faith. We usually think maturity means having it all figured out. James suggests that we don't have everything figured out. We're on the road to maturity when we realize how needy we are. Trials remind us that we are dependent on the Lord. They expose us, humble us, and grow us in unique ways. In success and trial, the Lord is working to make us more like Jesus. Of course, it's easy to be grateful for success. We all love to do well at something. But I'm learning that trials are just as important.

When the manager encouraged me to figure out my game in 2009, at first I saw the season as a painful trial. Over time, the Lord slowly began to show me the purpose of it all. Now I'm actually grateful for the experience. I learned a lot about myself and the Lord during that season. I learned how trials expose our hearts. They reveal what we value and worship—and that's a good thing, because we are so prone to worship the wrong thing. If the manager's comments had crushed me, it would have been evident that I cared more about baseball than anything else. I do love baseball, but it's not worthy of my worship. Only the Lord deserves that.

I'm tremendously grateful for the past few years. I think I've grown up a lot, and trials have a lot to do with my maturation. Life is full of trials, and we will all inevitably face them. They offer us great opportunities to learn more about ourselves and, ultimately, to learn more about the Lord. God is merciful to walk with us through trials. He loves us enough to never let us stay the same. Whether you are currently dealing with a trial or enjoying a success, I encourage you to welcome whatever the Lord is doing in your life. Trust that He will use it to conform you to the image of Christ. It is never easy to be humbled and put in our place. But we're not everything. God is merciful to keep reminding us of that.

# 23

# Twenty-one and in the Playoffs

Clayton

**Senior year consisted of three things: Ping-Pong, XBox and baseball.** When we weren't in Robert's backhouse playing *Halo*, we were at the Dickensons' house playing Ping-Pong. Generally speaking, I think my friends would consider me a pretty laid-back guy, but that was not the case when I had a paddle in hand. I started establishing my Ping-Pong dominance at an early age. That last semester of high school was as good as it gets. Those were the glory days for my buddies and me. Unfortunately, life had to move on.

After high school graduation, things changed in a hurry. Ellen left the day after graduation to start summer school in College Station, Texas. Then I jumped on a plane to chase a dream that had become a reality. By God's grace, I was going to play baseball professionally. The years of Minor League ball flew by, and as quickly as I could deflate my air mattress, I was in a Dodger uniform. In the blink of an eye, I was facing batters I had grown up watching on SportsCenter. I used to mimic their swings, and now I was trying to get them out. Beneath a calm demeanor, I was just a kid with sweaty palms who could hardly believe he was a Big League baseball player.

My first two years in the Major Leagues were awesome. Playing for Joe Torre in the beginning will have an impact on me for the rest of my career. He saw potential in me but was careful not to rush my development. Mr. Torre took me out of games early so that I didn't risk wearing out my arm. Even though I was stubborn and often asked him to leave me in the game, I trusted that he knew best. Looking back, I am so grateful for his discernment. Under his management, the Dodgers made it to the playoffs both years, and I loved the whole experience. During the playoffs of my rookie season, the Dodgers used me as a relief pitcher coming out of the bullpen—just enough experience to get my feet wet. The taste of post-season baseball was amazing. You don't realize how hard it is to make the playoffs until you're on a team with guys who have played for a while and never gotten there. They help you see what a privilege it is to play into October.

Most of my friends celebrated their twenty-first birthdays with all of the style that college life has to offer. I turned 21 and drank my first beer in the middle of spring training. I had tried to keep my age under the radar, but my teammates figured it out. They were quite amused that I was so young and still struggled with the occasional voice crack. I finally turned 21, but I was still the youngest player on the team. It was a significant birthday for me. I pitched the game on my birthday and even topped it off with my first home run. If only spring training home runs could count! Only a couple of weeks later, I received an invitation from Mr. Torre to accompany him on the team plane back to Los Angeles for a benefit dinner. We were joined on the plane by Dodger pitching legend Sandy Koufax. For two hours between Phoenix and L.A., I had the privilege of talking to Mr. Koufax and learning from the wisdom he had acquired during his renowned career. Meeting and spending time with such an accomplished player of the game was incredible.

We went to the playoffs again that fall. This time, I was handed the ball to start Game 1 in the series against the Philadelphia Phillies. My opponent: Cole Hamels. There was a lot of media hype surrounding the game. Two great clubs were going head-to-head for a chance to go deeper into the playoffs. The thought of starting in the playoffs against Hamels was surreal, but I convinced myself that I was up for the challenge. When the media starts talking, I have learned to listen with more discernment. Hype isn't always good for a starting pitcher, especially when you're 21. But in the days leading up to the first playoff start, I tried to focus on the task at hand and not let all the hype get to me.

I took the mound that night the same way I do every night— with butterflies in my stomach and too much adrenaline to contain. I was fairly confident that I was equipped to handle whatever came my way. I was excited about the opportunity. But then reality quickly set in. Guys were hitting my pitches hard. I walked a few batters. Before I knew it, I was out of the game. Hamels was dominant, and I got the loss. We lost the series just a few days later.

It was humbling to be on stage and have the spotlight—and then fail to deliver. I didn't realize it until after the loss, but I felt an enormous pressure to perform. People were watching me, and I assumed that they expected as much from me as I expected from myself. I felt like I had let everyone down, including my teammates. When I needed to perform, I didn't come through.

Since that loss in the playoffs, I have had other bad games, to say the least. But I learned something that season, and that lesson has helped me deal graciously with the games I've lost since then. I'm trying to see all these bumps in the road as part of the process of becoming the man and pitcher I want to be. There's always room for growth, and the low points keep me humble and hungry. I sometimes wish the Lord were not quite so faithful to remind me, "Clayton, you don't have it all figured out." But that's a really good place to be. When I lost to the Phillies in the playoffs, I was only 21 years old. I had a lot to learn, but I had plenty of time to learn it. I didn't have it all figured out, and I didn't need to convince myself that I did.

I am grateful that the Lord teaches me about humility. All the lessons keep me dependent on Him. People often say that the Lord won't give us anything we can't handle. But I see it in a different way. If I could handle everything that came my way, I would deal with it on my own. I wouldn't need the Lord or His grace in my life. It's really not about what I can handle. It's about how much I need Him. So those moments of choking on the big stage are really just gracious reminders that I'll never be able to do it on my own. Honestly, as discouraging as that sounds, it's exactly what I want to remember. I do believe that the Lord won't give me anything I can't handle . . . with His help. Christ is sufficient, and I never want to think that I can make it without Him.

I'm also learning to give myself time to grow up. It takes awhile to figure out how to pitch in the Big Leagues against batters who have been playing baseball for years. I want to stay hungry and work hard, and I realize that working hard is a blessing. Having the ability to work and to pour myself into something is huge for me. Especially in this world, we find so much purpose and value in what we do. Work doesn't define us, but it's a big part of who we are. I work hard, not because I am defined by my job, but because I work for God's glory.

I realize now that it's a rare privilege to make it to the playoffs. It's so rare, in fact, that when you're there, you should fight with everything you have to win. Today I am grateful for games we won to clinch a series, and I'm also grateful for the games in which we got close but came up short. Those experiences keep my competitive heart humble. Being 21 and in the playoffs was remarkable. Through those games and in the seasons since, I have learned that God uses our losses and trials as much as He uses our wins and successes. When the Lord humbles us, we remember that we need a Savior. We only have to look at Jesus to realize how God can bring beautiful things out of even the worst moments. The cross seems like the greatest defeat, but now we know that Jesus went through that suffering to win the ultimate victory over sin and death. If God can do that with the cross, He can do something beautiful with any trial.

After a long season of winning and sometimes losing, it's sweet to head home for the off-season. The glory days of high school are gone but not forgotten. The same buddies are waiting for me in Dallas every off-season. We still play the occasional *Halo* game in Robert's backhouse. We still head to the Dickensons' for a rousing Ping-Pong tournament. The trash talk is always good, and the winner has never changed!

# 24

## THAT THEY WOULD SEE THE LORD

Ellen

**I've watched a lot of baseball in my life—probably much more than most girls my age.** I've been watching Clayton play for nine years, ever since we started dating. Before Clayton, I went to all of my brothers' games. So baseball has been a part of my life for a long time. After all of these years, I can't say that my favorite part is the actual game. It's entertaining to watch and be a part of, but it isn't the best part. My favorite part is getting to watch Clayton.

When we were in high school, I never imagined that so much of my life would revolve around pitching rotations and pitch counts. I also never would have guessed that watching Clayton play baseball would be such a walk of faith for me. Clayton is a pretty calm and collected person. His emotions never get too high or too low. I'm grateful for this because, as my family would tell you, I tend to live in superlatives. Clayton is the perfect balance for me. When he is pitching, game days are pretty quiet around our home. We wake up, have breakfast and hang out until it's time to head to the field. He is normally calm and fairly reserved on those mornings. He's focused on the game, which keeps him from getting distracted by all the hype that surrounds it. He's also doing what he loves to do, so there's nothing to be nervous about. He reassures me of this when I drive him to the stadium. We roll the car windows down for Clayton's game day ritual—blasting some good Beyoncé tunes. He always seems to be doing great, and that encourages me to get to that same peaceful place.

Each time he steps onto the mound for a game, I find myself praying the same prayer. Maybe it's become a bit of a routine. But beyond that, I find myself praying the same things because I really long for them to be true. I always start with gratitude. Clayton and I talk all the time about how every good gift comes from the Lord (see Jas. 1:17). Everything good in our lives is from Him, without exception. This includes Clayton's gift to play baseball. He works hard to perfect it, but at the end of the day, Clayton's gift is God-given. I start with praise because I've got to remember what is true. God gives His children good things. As a result, I ask the Lord to use Clayton's gift to point people to Him—I ask that they would see the Lord. I pray that the people watching would see the Lord in the way that Clayton pitches and in how he conducts himself during the game. None of us is perfect, and a bad game can make anyone upset. But even in trials, I ask the Lord to give Clayton grace to conduct himself in a manner worthy of Him. I know that's what Clayton wants as well.

God created everything on earth to bring Himself glory. Have you ever thought of that? Everything in nature shouts praise to the Lord. I see that so clearly when I stand before the roaring ocean or in the middle of the snow-capped mountains in Colorado. God made the world so beautifully and masterfully that it cannot help but sing His praises. God's people also bring Him glory, as they are the pinnacle of His creation. I see this so clearly when I watch other people chasing their purpose and dreams in the life the Lord has given them. God is glorified in my sister's dream to write and in my parents' dedication to give back to our community. He equips His people with passions and dreams that ultimately make Him look great.

My world has been turned upside down by witnessing this truth in Africa. I've never seen people more joyful, content in the Lord and grateful for life. I hope that the people in Zambia see the Lord in me. I know that I have been changed as I see the Lord in them. But you don't have to be in Africa to bring God glory. Clayton takes his position in the middle of a pitching mound in Los Angeles, California, or some other city in America—and God gets the glory. I pray for that with every pitch. It's great when the team wins, but I know that it's bigger than that. It can be and should be about something as big as God's glory.

People are attracted to people with passion. You can see that throughout history. Passionate people make headlines. Sometimes passion and zeal go awry, and horrific things like war are the result. But other times, passion reveals the Lord at work. Clayton loves baseball more than anyone I've ever met. Baseball has never been "work" for him because he loves every minute of it. Doing his job is not a drag for him. It's a tremendous joy. When people notice that we love what we do, they begin to ask questions. They question the hope that we have, because in our world, joyful passion sometimes looks bizarre. I always pray for Clayton to be joyful knowing that he is right in the midst of the Lord's purpose for him. I think about Colossians 1:10, in which Paul prays, "That you may live a life worthy of the Lord and may please him in every way: bearing fruit in every good work, growing in the knowledge of God." When we walk in a manner worthy of the Lord, people can't help but see Christ. My prayer is that people would see Christ in Clayton.

The Lord uses all sorts of things to draw us closer to Him. For me, watching Clayton play baseball is one of them. It was incredible to go to Africa and watch the Lord use Clayton and baseball to draw kids near to Him. As I watched Clayton play catch with children in Zambia, I saw the Lord at work. I prayed that the children would see it, too. God uses us and our gifts for great purposes. The greatest purpose of all is His glory. During a game, you can find me in the stands. Sometimes I'm watching contentedly; other times I'm hoping that the game doesn't go into extra innings. Being in L.A., of course I'm hoping for a celebrity spotting. But you can be sure that I'm praying for the same things every time. I always hope for a Dodger win. But I'm most prayerful that people would see the Lord in Clayton.

# 25

## DRAW NEAR TO GOD

Ellen

**People come in and out of our lives on a daily basis.** Some come and stay for only a season, but others remain part of our lives forever. On rare occasions, we meet people for the first time and feel like we have already known them for a lifetime. Years and distance don't seem to make any difference. There is a shared heartbeat, and the connection is undeniable. That is how I felt the first time I met Hope. Our story is just beginning, but she has already changed my life.

I met Hope during the summer of 2010, when I made my fourth trip to Africa. She was 10 years old at the time but looked as if she had lived much longer. Hope is an orphan in Zambia. The first time I saw Hope, her head was down and her shoulders were hunched over. She didn't want to look at me and seemed too shy even to smile. She caught my attention more than any child ever has—I'm still not sure why. Her eyes were so swollen that she could barely open them. After a visit to the nurse, I learned so much more about my new friend. She rolled her pant leg up to reveal a ghastly leg wound. A few tests confirmed that Hope was HIV positive. Unfortunately, this is a story that you hear every day in Zambia.

The orphans of Zambia are vulnerable to disease, poverty, suffering and loss in a way that we can hardly fathom in America. Pain is the norm, and death is an everyday reality. Children lack hope, love and joy—they've been taught by their circumstances to face life without emotion. Yet, for four years now, I have watched these kids come to life as they heard the good news of Jesus Christ. I have seen their hearts catch fire when they first heard of their Father in heaven. I have also witnessed the Lord heal their broken hearts as they shared the pain of losing a parent. Human beings can never be completely calloused to pain, no matter how hard we try to forget it. As a result, we all look for and try to cling to something consistent. By God's grace, I have seen these children cling to their faith in Jesus. You know how we all wish for faith like a child? Since meeting kids like Hope, I have prayed for faith like a Zambian. Though I had only known Hope for a few minutes, when I heard her diagnosis, my heart broke like I had known her for years. Sadly, in many parts of Zambia, people don't care enough about orphans to test them for HIV. When I found out that Hope was infected, it was a gut punch of emotion. I had been told that most of the children I would meet would be HIV positive. But for the first time, I looked into the eyes of a child, knowing she would have to suffer a lifetime with a disease she did not deserve. None of it made sense to me. I was angry about the epidemic that plagues these children. I have never felt more urgency to pray, to preach the gospel, or to hold a child who needed a parent. The next day, I sat with Hope for over an hour, and we talked about Jesus. One of the most frustrating things was not being able to speak Nyanga, Hope's tribal language. I prayed that my words would be clear, and that the Lord would move her heart to grasp the gospel. Hope could barely wrap her mind around the thought of a heavenly Father. We had funny exchanges of miscommunication. Then we looked together at an Evangecube—a tool for explaining what Jesus did to save us. Suddenly, as we were looking at it, I could tell that something clicked for Hope. She began to explain the gospel back to me in Nyanga with hand motions. I watched with tear-filled eyes. A simple yet staggering truth brought freedom to her life. Christ made her feel significant. The good news that Jesus loved her and came to die for her sins changed everything.

Hope and I spent the next few days getting to know each other. With the help of other Zambians, we began to devise a plan to get her the medical attention she desperately needed. Since our first encounter, I have watched Hope's transformation. No one laughs or gives hugs like Hope. She captivates her entire group of friends with her sense of humor. She is a beautiful picture of how the gospel can change a life from the inside out. For the first time, Hope felt significant. She had a purpose and a place in the world. The change in her heart is evident in the joy on her face.

When it was time for me to leave that summer, I felt like I was leaving half of my heart in Zambia. I have had a similar feeling every summer, but this time was different. It was like someone knocked the wind out of me when I had to say goodbye. I was leaving Hope, and I felt the weight of her physical, medical and spiritual needs. I was afraid that if I didn't provide for her in those areas, no one else would. I felt so helpless and defeated. Over the course of my trip, I had written to Clayton and told him about Hope. Without hesitation, he gave me the wonderful gift of offering to help sponsor Hope and contribute toward her needs. That was something we could do—and yet, I didn't feel like it was enough. I wanted to do so much more for that child. I wished I could take her home and meet her needs on every level. I wished Clayton could get to know her, because I knew that he would love her as much as I did. I wanted so much to give her a different life and change her world.

As I flew home that summer, my heart sank. It was breaking for Hope, and I felt the incredible urge to fix and even control the situation. During that trip, the Lord put a passage on my heart that convicted me and gave me greater hope for Hope:

> I thank my God every time I remember you. In all my prayers for all of you, I always pray with joy because of your partnership in the gospel from the first day until now, being confident of this, that he who began a good work in you will carry it on to completion until the day of Christ Jesus. It is right for me to feel this way about all of you, since I have you in my heart; for whether I am in chains or defending and confirming the gospel, all of you share in God's grace with me. God can testify how I long for all of you with the affection of Christ Jesus (Phil. 1:3-8).

I am learning how to give up control. I knew I couldn't save Hope on my own. On the flight home, I realized how beautiful it was to plant seeds in Hope's life. The Lord would continue His work in her until it was time for her to go home to be with Jesus.

I didn't bring Jesus into her life. He had been with her since the day she was born. I simply pointed her to Jesus. Now I looked to Him to continue to move in her heart long after I left. It was a sweet privilege to show Hope that God had been there all along. During the few days we'd had together, we had talked about the nearness of God, and I read her a verse from James:

> Submit yourselves therefore to God. Resist the devil, and he will flee from you. Draw near to God, and he will draw near to you (Jas. 4:7-8, *ESV*).

Draw near to God, and He will draw near to you. I needed to hear that for myself, and I needed to hear that for Hope. Sometimes God's Word hits us right between the eyes, because it says exactly what we need to hear. In that moment, I needed the reminder that God is near—not only to me, but also to my friends in Zambia, and perhaps especially to Hope. The reality that I couldn't fix Hope or her world humbled me. I couldn't even make sure she got her next meal or the medication for her leg. I flew home feeling helpless—and that is when I discovered that helpless is a sweet place to be.

We often think too highly of ourselves and too little of God. I was looking to my own strength and resources to care for Hope. As I flew across the ocean back to Texas, the knowledge that everything I had was vastly insufficient discouraged me. But as I considered this passage from James, I remembered the sufficiency of Christ. I needed the same message I had been sharing with Hope for a week. Christ is enough! Our heavenly Father loves us, and He is able to care for each and every need. As I wrestled with this passage, it brought me new life. Even though I live in Dallas, Texas, and Hope lives in Lusaka, Zambia, the Lord is big enough to bridge the distance.

As I began to draw near to God, trusting in His provision for my own life, I noticed His presence in new and astounding ways. So I began to pray the same thing for Hope. I prayed that she would draw near to God and find Him to be more than enough for her needs. The gift of God's nearness changed me that summer. The Father's love for Hope was deeper, wider, longer and higher than my love for her could ever be. Because of that, I could be sure that He would watch over her every need. I thought I needed nothing more than for the Lord to take care of Hope. But in the midst of teaching me about Hope, He began teaching me about me. The nearness of God is overwhelming. He changes me as I think about Hope. He changes me as I look at my own life. The Lord is worthy of my full confidence, and His nearness brings me great hope.

# 26

# WORK AT IT WITH ALL YOUR HEART

Clayton

**I found myself sitting on the edge of my seat so I wouldn't miss a single word that he said.** His voice was barely above a whisper, so I leaned in. I noticed his hands. They were worn with age and weathered by time. I thought about the thousands of basketballs he had picked up. Beyond that, I thought about the millions of lives he had touched. He was 97 years old at the time. Though his words were few and quiet, I could tell that he was as sharp as a tack.

As we ate dinner, he shared thoughts and encouragement. When you sit across the table from a living legend, you try not to blink, for fear you'll miss something great. He graciously answered our questions, taking time to think through each response. He would listen and then pause. I held my breath, curious to hear what he would say next. Then he would respond—slowly, intent on relaying his thought with care and precision.

Someone at the table raised his hand with a question. "What is the most important part of life?" I leaned in again. The coach didn't seem to need a moment to think about his answer. Instead, he smiled and, without pause, responded: "Faith is the most important thing in your life and always should be." I relaxed back into my chair. *Faith*, I thought. After a lifetime of success, awards and even fame, he said faith mattered most. As dinner ended that night, I went up to him, thanking him for his time. He shook my hand and looked me right in the eye. I think he knew what I was thinking. He seemed to understand my new world of playing a professional sport better than I did. In a world filled with opportunities, I would be faced with the challenge of making something the most important aspect of my life. It could be anything. He suggested faith. I walked out of the restaurant that night wanting my faith to take center stage. I prayed that I would have the courage to live a life like he did.

John Wooden is one of the most legendary basketball icons of all time. He was named to the Basketball Hall of Fame as both a coach and a player. One of the most revered college coaches ever, he shepherded teams at UCLA to 10 national championships in a 12-year period. Seven of these championships were consecutive. Coach Wooden's methods of leadership, including the Pyramid of Success, continue to be an inspiration to millions today. He was the wisest person I have ever talked to in my life. Each time he spoke, a lifetime of experiences, hardships and joys came pouring out. He spoke with integrity and a great desire to pass along something worthwhile to the next generation. I could tell that his life had never been about himself. His remarkable and historic career had been focused on the Lord and on loving others in the Lord. Coach Wooden knew what it was like to be offered all of the riches in the world. He had reached unbelievable heights of success in coaching basketball. Even so, at the end of it all, he said assuredly that faith was greater than everything else. In his list of priorities, faith always came before championships, trophies and Hall of Fame status. He made faith the most important thing in his life. I have tremendous respect for Coach Wooden and consider it an extraordinary privilege that I got to meet him face to face.

Sharing a meal with him was a significant moment for me. I had the opportunity to meet a legend who had been always a distant inspiration to me. My coaches had often quoted him, and our high school leadership class highlighted him as a prime example of a phenomenal leader. Growing up, I knew exactly who Coach Wooden was. I never dreamed that I would actually get to meet him. His answer to that one question stays with me. I am grateful for his perspective on the importance of keeping a faith-centered life. When Coach Wooden passed away in 2010, I considered the incredible gift of having gotten to meet him. He had achieved so much in the world of sports, but in a way that looked very different from the norm. Coach worked hard for the Lord, not for man. His sights were set first on faith in God—and only after that, on the next championship.

When I was a junior in high school, I came across a passage of Scripture that really stood out to me. For the first time that I remember, Colossians 3:23 caught my attention: "Whatever you do, work at it with all your heart, as working for the Lord, not for men." I read it in a devotional book that year, and it has been my favorite verse ever since. It made a lot of sense to me at the time. I thought about how I should work at whatever I'm doing with all of my heart. Even in high school, I began to see the benefits of doing God-glorifying work. This included schoolwork and, of course, baseball.

I never knew that baseball would be something I would get to play past high school. There was always that hope, but it was nothing that I really spent a lot of time thinking about. As junior year rolled around, I began to consider seriously that I might have the opportunity to play at the next level. That goal inspired me. I wanted to work hard to get to play in college. As I put so much effort toward baseball, it began to be a walk of faith for me. I was working hard, but I worried that it wouldn't be enough. Baseball could be my avenue to go to a great college. The thought of failing and not measuring up put a knot in my stomach. I think the Lord dropped Colossians 3:23 in my lap at the perfect time. As the apostle Paul instructed, I decided to work for the Lord and trust Him to provide the next step. I know now that the Lord answered my prayers in a way I never could have imagined. Trusting the Lord with my future was one of the most liberating and rewarding things I've ever done.

As I began to operate according to the new perspective of working for the Lord, it changed the way I interacted with people. I had the opportunity to become a captain on the baseball team at Highland Park. It's sometimes hard to figure out how to be a leader among your peers. I didn't want to stand out so much that I wasn't one of the guys. But I also wanted to fill the role that the coach had assigned to me. I decided that I wanted to lead by doing what I needed to do individually. I hoped that if I did that, others would follow my example. I learned that people often respond well when you exemplify leadership instead of assuming authority. I came to find out that people are encouraged to step up by themselves. Then others will naturally become leaders as well. I wanted my teammates to see that I had a strong work ethic and that I was working for the Lord. It's one thing to talk about the Lord. It's another thing to demonstrate that you're living for the Lord.

In the Major Leagues, the same principle holds true: It's one thing to say what I believe, and it's a completely different thing to live it out. People pay attention to how we choose to live. People evaluate what we really believe as they observe our actions. As a student leader in high school, I wanted people to see the fulfillment that I found in working hard for the Lord. How I lived for the Lord mattered in high school, and it still matters today. When we work with all our hearts for the Lord, our eyes are fixed on Him. We're not working for the people around us, but sooner or later, they start to notice something different about us. Then we have an opportunity to tell them why we live the way we live.

Working with all your heart for the Lord brings incredible meaning to life. It doesn't matter what you're doing, where you are in life, or what activity or sport you love. You have an opportunity to work hard and see the Lord's blessing. God has a greater purpose for each of us. When we believe that, we start to find incredible motivation to work hard. It can be as simple as doing your homework or as profound as seeing the Lord open someone's eyes for the first time. As I worked hard at baseball practice in high school, each day was a tiny step toward the great plan the Lord had for me. God has a purpose for your life. As you work hard for the Lord, exactly where you are, you'll begin to see that His purpose for your life is pretty incredible.

By senior year at Highland Park, I knew that I could play in college. That was an awesome feeling. But God had something else in mind. On draft day, 2006, hundreds of baseball players from around the country were going to get drafted. I hoped to be one of them. When the Dodgers called, that was an unbelievable moment. I had worked hard in high school because I was hopeful that there was something more. I had also found satisfaction in working for the Lord and trusting Him to handle the rest. I never imagined that His plan for me could be so amazing.

Coach Wooden hit the nail on the head that night at dinner. Faith first, hard work second. His life made one thing very clear:

When your faith in the Lord is the priority, working with all your heart is richly satisfying. After living 97 years, Coach Wooden told me that nothing was more important than faith. I expect I'll have to live my entire life to know fully the truth of that statement. But it didn't take long to figure out that Coach knew exactly what he was talking about. He had lived a life focused on the Lord. I hope that one day, years from now, I can look back at my own life and see the same thing.

# 27

# ALREADY BUT NOT YET

Ellen

**Clayton and I never talked about marriage in high school. Never ever.** We were both on the same page: Nothing could be more awkward than talking about the future when we hadn't even gone to senior prom. It just didn't make any sense. In fact, the trendy thing to do was break up after high school graduation. No one wanted to carry baggage into the next chapter of life. They wanted a fresh start. So it looked strange to some people when Clayton and I agreed to stick with it. To us, breaking up would mean losing a best friend as well as a boyfriend or girlfriend. We wanted to see if we could make it work before throwing in the towel. We decided to give a long-distance relationship a try. If things didn't work out down the road, at least we took the chance. Our conversation at the end of high school was really that simple. We didn't talk about future plans. We just talked about taking it one step at a time.

I'm really grateful that things played out that way. We agreed not to get ahead of ourselves, but just to enjoy the ride. As a result, my college years were some of the best years of my life. I think Clayton would say the same thing about his experience in the Minors and then starting in the Majors. We were living two separate lives. But we also had each other as a reminder of home. We both felt free to enjoy exactly where we were without the pressure of future promises.

People start making assumptions when two people have been dating for many years—they assume you're in for the long haul. That thought never really crossed my mind until I was near the end of college. Suddenly, college was almost over, and the rest of my life stood before me like a blank page. That was an unsettling feeling. For the first time in my life, I faced an unknown abyss. After middle school, I knew there was high school. After that, I knew that college was right around the corner. But as I started my senior year at Texas A&M University, it hit me: I had no idea what the next step would be. I didn't know what I wanted to do as a career, and I wasn't sure where things would land with Clayton. It didn't make sense to find a job in Dallas if I was going to be moving to Los Angeles. Then again, I didn't want to bank my whole future on a guy who was just my boyfriend at the time.

I visited Clayton a few times during the summer before my senior year. We had some great conversations about the future. Marriage had never been an option or a topic of conversation until that year. Suddenly, we didn't feel crazy talking about it. It made sense because the timing was right. Clayton saw that season as the "game changer" for us. He was testing the waters to see if the next step—engagement—made sense. Before I went back for my final year of college, we had a wonderful summer together. I spent a lot of time in L.A., and I think we both realized how perfect it felt to be in the same city again. Over the years, we had great consistency. We could go two months without seeing each other and then pick right back up where we left off. Everything fit. I knew that it was right because I was a better person when I was with him.

As the baseball season came to a close, Clayton made his way back to Texas. I figured the next few months could be significant, but I wasn't sure that a proposal was inevitable. Clayton was pretty quiet about it. In fact, he didn't seem to want to talk about it at all. I misread those signals and assumed that he had no idea what he was doing. Little did I know that he had a plan, and things were falling perfectly into place. Clayton was already part of our family, so he had the connections to get things rolling. He knew that my sister, Ann, was my best friend and closest confidant. She had talked me through every up and down of growing up together and prayerfully encouraged my relationship with Clayton. She has been like an older sister to him for years, and I swear they turn into 10-year-olds when they are with each other. This usually means teaming up against me. Clayton took Ann to lunch and shared his vision for an engagement. She later told me that he sat across the table from her without even touching his sandwich. She knew that something had to be going on! As plans moved forward for a pre-Christmas proposal, I became convinced that it was never going to happen. Clayton and my family gave me no reason to believe that anything was going on. He had me completely fooled.

The night of the proposal, I sat in my room crying before Clayton arrived to take me to dinner. I was frustrated and convinced that he was totally missing the opportunity to move things forward in our relationship. It made sense for us to be together! Why was he acting so oblivious? Did he really think that long-distance dating was fun? I dried my eyes just in time to walk down the stairs and meet him. I tried to act like nothing was wrong. Then I noticed he had on a brand-new suit. Beyond that, I was shocked to see that his patchy beard was gone. In the front driveway sat a white stretch limousine. For all my emotions and frustrations, I still had no idea what was going on. He took me on the perfect date that night. We toured around our hometown of Highland Park, looking at Christmas lights, and then ended up downtown for dinner. I just assumed that this was all he had planned—a wonderful date together, but nothing more.

As we drove back to my house, the limousine driver made a stop at Clayton's townhome. Clayton said he had something to pick up. I remained completely clueless. As we walked up to the front door, I noticed a glow coming from inside. He opened the door, and Christmas music came bellowing out. I stepped into a winter wonderland. His home was filled with Christmas—lights, snow, garland and trees. We walked upstairs, where the scenery got even better. A huge Christmas tree stood proudly in the middle of the room. The tree was covered with bright ornaments and topped off with a red bow that cascaded from the top all the way down. Smaller trees were scattered around the room, and dry-ice snow covered the floor. It was stunning, and I was completely shocked. I turned around, amazed by the detailed planning and preparation that had obviously gone into all of this. Christmas exploded out of every corner, and my dream was coming true. Beneath the tree sat a single present. As I opened it, I found a tiny Santa Claus figurine. In his hands, he held a small velvet box—the perfect size for a ring.

That moment changed my life. Through tears, I looked at Clayton in disbelief. The boy who had asked me out in the middle of passing period at age 14 had come up with the most perfect, beautiful proposal I could ever imagine. Clayton asked me to marry him! I was engaged to my best friend. He really did know what he was doing! As the music rang through the house, I thought about the goodness of God to us for so many years. In His plan for us, He knew that we would be together. He made us for each other. When our paths crossed at age 14, it was an "already but not yet" moment. We would end up together . . . but not yet. His timing is perfect.

We drove back to my parents' house that night, and I could hardly wait to see my family. I had no idea that the gathering would include so many more. The house was full. Friends and family had driven in from all over to share the moment. As I walked into the house, I was blown away by the outpouring of love from so many dear people. We celebrated into the night and quickly began making plans for a wedding the following off-season. Even a wedding has to play by the rules of baseball.

Seven years of dating was well worth the wait. When I said "yes" to Clayton's proposal, I was looking at my best friend. We knew life together would be great, because we had years of proof. We were always meant to be together. I think that's why things worked out so beautifully. We can't mess up the Lord's will for our lives. Clayton and I grew up together. Moving toward engagement made sense, and so did living life together in L.A. after the wedding. I wanted to be wherever he was. As we moved into engagement, there was a new kind of "already but not yet." We would soon be married, but not yet. The Lord had more to teach us as we waited and grew through another baseball season together. But this time, there was a light at the end of the tunnel. We would be married in December! It was a long road from awkward teenagers to a married couple, but we're so grateful for how the Lord wrote our story. We felt like we were in the middle of God's will, even when He kept us waiting awhile for His perfect timing.

# 28

# EVERY EXIT IS BLOCKED

Ellen

**It's rush hour in Dallas—the kind of traffic that makes you want to crank up the radio and hope you can drown out the noise of motors and honking.** After a long day of working and running errands, I'm at a standstill on the highway. Everyone is desperate to get somewhere—and fast—but no one is moving. Each driver has the same desire—to get out of traffic and arrive safely home. As I inch through traffic, I spot an exit ahead. I begin the crazy quest of crossing five lanes to get off the highway and find an easier route. Minutes later, I arrive at the exit and notice that it has been blocked. In fact, so is the next exit. And the next. A sign blinks overhead: "Every exit is blocked. Proceed forward." I take a deep breath as I realize that I'm on this road for the long haul. There is no way to veer to the left or the right. I certainly can't reverse with the traffic jam behind me. The only option is forward movement.

That's what marriage is like, our pastor told us. Marriage is like being on a highway with every exit blocked. Sometimes it gets tight and frustrating—like a rush-hour traffic jam. Other times there is clear sailing with not an obstacle in sight. But the key is remembering that there is no opportunity to exit. Whether you like it or not, you're stuck on the road. Our pastor back home in Texas is a dear friend, so naturally we were excited to ask him to officiate our wedding ceremony. We spent a few afternoons with him before our wedding for some premarital counseling. We talked through many different topics, and Clayton and I agree that our time with Dr. Ron Scates was a blessing. His illustration of rush-hour traffic hit us right between the eyes. We loved that thought and agreed that it was a profound way to think about our new marriage.

Our culture lacks a serious perspective on commitment. Just about every television show will offer supporting evidence that commitment doesn't matter to most people. Whether it's in a job or with friends, or even in a marriage, commitment seems to be a loose term. There is always an exit strategy. When you feel like something doesn't work for you anymore, you just get off that road. We decided after our meeting with Dr. Scates that we wanted to be different in our marriage and life together. We talked about how cool it would be to redefine what a marriage could look like. The first step was to get rid of any thoughts of exiting. Like our pastor's symbolic highway, we decided to block every exit. We knew that things wouldn't always be easy, but together we agreed that our marriage would be for a lifetime. Making that promise to each other so early on has changed the way we live out our marriage one day at a time.

Now, some might think we are too young and naïve to know what we're talking about. However, I like to think that we are full of hope and dependence on the Lord. By God's grace, marriage is possible even in a broken world where commitment is so shaky. Marriage is possible because it is important to God. He designed marriage to paint a picture of the love Jesus has for His people, the Church. That love never fades or breaks. A God-glorifying marriage is the Lord's way of showing the world what His love for us looks like. That means that marriage is a big deal and should be treated as such.

Clayton and I developed what we call our "game plan for marriage." While we were engaged, we had the opportunity to talk to a number of married couples and friends. We were seeking wisdom and vision for a godly marriage. The most helpful insight that we received was that a marriage will never be perfect, because two imperfect people are tied up in it. But a marriage can be joyful, fulfilling, and bring glory to God. I guess people are more prone to talk about how marriage is hard. Few people in our world talk about the greatness of two people finding the Lord to be abundantly gracious in a marriage. We want to set the record straight.

Our game plan isn't too complicated. It mainly highlights the things we want to be about as a couple. More than anything, we want to be about the Lord. Many people in this world will only know who Jesus is by looking at those who claim to be His followers.

Clayton and I want our friends and family to see Jesus, and we hope that our marriage will help them recognize that God is good. We both desire to know Christ more and more each day. Having that as a foundation for marriage can really change the way you live life together.

We want to be about other people. It's amazing to see how the Lord has given us friendships, baseball and mission work in Africa to focus our attention on others. Relationships matter to us—showing people the love of Jesus matters even more. Nothing brings us greater joy than involving our friends and family in our life and marriage. In some unique ways, our marriage is on display, simply because of where the Lord has planted us. Our day-to-day life is filled with people, and we wouldn't have it any other way. With all the opportunities the Lord has given us, we hope to be focused on others in our marriage.

We want our marriage to be about pointing each other to Christ. Clayton's faithful presence in my life reminds me how the Lord has been by my side every step of the way. Most of my memorable life has been with Clayton. I am so proud of his accomplishments and the way his humility stands out above everything else. But most of all, I'm grateful for his heart for the Lord. I pray that Clayton will never love me more than he loves the Lord. Likewise, I pray that I will always love the Lord first and Clayton second. We long to be about pointing each other to Jesus.

Finally, our game plan is to enjoy every moment of life with each other. Even though we're married and finally getting to spend more time in the same city, our relationship can still feel long-distance. Clayton is on the road every other week playing away games, and we want to make sure that we never take a moment together for granted. Laughter is one of the greatest gifts the Lord has blessed us with in our marriage. There is no better medicine for an argument than being able to laugh. We share a humor that no one else would understand. But my parents can attest to the number of nights when they fell asleep to us belly-laughing downstairs while we were in high school. I am sure that the Lord finds great delight when we enjoy life with the people around us.

A game plan is important in every sport. If you don't have a plan, you don't know what to do when you get in the game and things start to happen. When people get married, things always start to happen. Life happens, and we need a game plan if we're going to walk through it any differently than the rest of the world does. Clayton and I don't have things all figured out. I know that we never will. But I am confident that we are ready for the journey ahead. The exits are blocked, and I'm strapped in next to my best friend. We're sure that it will be a challenging, funny and rewarding ride.

# 29

# BREATHING LIFE INTO OUR PRAYERS

Clayton

**I was standing right next to him in the middle of Sunday worship.** Isaac sang each song like it might be his last time to sing. Rich tones and a beautiful Zambian accent rang out from his small body and echoed off every wall. I could tell that he meant every word that came out of his mouth—"Tout le me Totela" (to God alone be the glory). He held his hands over his head while his feet danced to the beat of the song. I couldn't imagine seeing someone worship like this back at home. People would be uncomfortable witnessing such a scene.

As the singing subsided, the music continued through the crowd's hums. My friend Isaac began to pray aloud. I found myself standing there with my eyes wide open. I looked around and saw the most incredible picture of worship I have ever seen in my life. The Zambians were swaying back and forth, keeping the steady beat of the continued hums. Some bowed their heads, while others lifted their faces high—as if they anticipated that the voice of God would respond in that moment. I could tell that they were serious about worshiping the Lord. It looked as though they thought that meeting with the Lord was the work of their lives. Ellen had always told me that she thought worship in Zambia was a picture of what worship in heaven would look like. In that moment, I knew what she was talking about. They weren't in a hurry to get somewhere else. Isaac prayed for a long time, praising the Lord for His goodness and His mercy to sinners. As I listened to his words, it was as if I were hearing the gospel for the first time. His prayer was clear and filled with gospel-centered thoughts and confessions. He spoke with great intensity as he asked for forgiveness and acknowledged his sin. His sorrow over his sin turned to joy as he proclaimed God's graciousness in sending a Savior.

With a loud, bellowing "AMEN!" the other Zambians chimed in with shouted hallelujahs. They proceeded to walk around, hugging one another. They included me in the hugs, too. Their passion blew me away. Isaac grabbed me by the shoulder and embraced me like he had known me forever. A big smile broke across his face, and the joy of the Lord just spilled right out of him. I told Isaac that it was amazing to hear someone pray with such zeal. He just laughed and said, "Ah, Americans! They are so weak in their prayers! God is all-powerful. Shout out to the Lord with thanks!" I knew exactly what he meant. That comment has changed the way I pray.

My visit to Africa with Ellen was an incredible experience. I have never seen anything like it. All the time we spent with Zambian friends and orphans changed my whole perspective. I finally got to meet Hope. After months of praying for her with Ellen, it was awesome to meet her face to face—an amazing answer to prayer. God began to breathe life into my prayers. I felt so foolish about the way I had been worshiping the Lord back home. The Zambians worshiped the same God I did, but they made Him look incredibly more valuable by the way they sang and prayed. They lived and worshiped like they knew their Maker and had a relationship with their Savior. We often act as if God is an obligation reserved for Sunday. I was convicted as I thought about America, where we often look for satisfaction everywhere but in the Lord.

Our Zambian friends didn't shame me into thinking that I was failing in my faith. Instead, they encouraged me to believe that Jesus deserved so much more. I was reminded of how little we actually need to be satisfied on earth. As Ellen and I walked through the communities one morning, hundreds of children surrounded us. Their formula for life is shockingly simple. If they have their basic needs met—food, water and shelter—they are joyful. In America, we search for worth and purpose in material things. The kids in Zambia run around with bare feet. They have one apple per day. They have a shabby roof over their heads. And they are the happiest people in the world! I think about that old hymn, "Great Is Thy Faithfulness." There is a lyric in that song that says, "All I have needed, Thy hand hath provided." Zambians really understand that. All they need has been taken care of by the Lord. I consider them richly blessed in not having all of the stuff we have in America. They understand what it means to be in "need." Beyond that, they understand the Lord's provision. In our culture, people who are considered less than wealthy yearn for the things they don't have. They long for more because they think that "things" will make them happy. It is completely the opposite in Africa, and I found that so refreshing. The people I met there have discovered the source of deeply satisfying joy—the Lord.

As we returned to America, I knew I didn't want to be the person I had been when I left. I didn't want to worship the same way, and I didn't want to pray the same way. I wanted to live differently because of what I saw in Zambia and learned from Isaac. Our culture in the States paints God into a very small corner. We like to keep Him in a neat little box where He can be contained and controlled. The Zambians invite God to affect every aspect of their lives. They worship Him with great fervor because they really do believe that He is powerful and merciful to them. We are missing it in America.

When I pray, it is hard not to think about Isaac. I remember watching him worship the Lord and wanting to feel the same things he felt. As believers, the way we love, revere and worship the Lord should inspire people to wonder what all the hype is about. Worshiping the Lord—in song, in prayer, or even in everyday life—should cause people to want to know the God we are praising. I was convicted in Africa that my life doesn't always accomplish that task. Lord willing, it will begin to look different. Sometimes we need to stand back to really get a good perspective on life. I stood in Africa, looking thousands of miles back at my life in America, and I wanted to change. The Lord's work in Africa breathed new life into my prayers and my life.

# 30

# WHEN PASSIONS COLLIDE

Clayton

**I didn't even recognize the person I had just married.** We had only been on Zambian soil for a few minutes before Ellen began speaking Nyanga. It's crazy when you hear someone you have known most of your life speaking a language you never knew existed. This city girl—who wouldn't touch a bug to save her life—was all of a sudden walking through dirt and slums as if she was finally home. With no make-up on, her hair pulled back, and holes in her jeans, she fearlessly took charge as we made our way through the darkest villages I have ever seen.

It had been a really long day. Twenty-two hours on a plane was no small feat for me. My legs were numb for two days afterwards. When we landed in Zambia, I knew that we had our work cut out for us. The trip involved two different activities—putting on a day camp for orphans and building classrooms at the Greenhill School in Zambia. The prospect of manual labor to build a classroom was exciting to me. Ever since we had booked our tickets to Zambia, I had been a little nervous. Ellen had been so many times before, but this was my first time to go with her. For years, she had told me stories and showed me pictures. Life looked and sounded really tough for the people in Zambia. I worried about feeling overwhelmed and not knowing what to do with it all. But manual labor—that was something I could do. I felt confident that at least I could contribute in that area. I didn't know how I would be able to help the children, but I was certain I could stir cement and move dirt around. As it turned out, we did a lot more than manual labor during our time in Africa—and the trip changed me far more than I ever could have expected.

I was also anxious about going to Africa in the middle of the off-season because I needed to stay on my training schedule. Even though we were home in Dallas for the holidays, I had a routine of working out and throwing the ball. I knew that a solid start to next season depended on my staying disciplined during my time away from the field. When I brought up these concerns to Ellen, she assured me that we would come up with a plan to make it all work. In the end, it worked out perfectly. I shipped my blue pitching tarp to Zambia ahead of me. If we could just figure out a way to hang that tarp, I could pitch every day, and that would cover it. When we landed in Zambia, a throng of incredible people, many of whom knew Ellen, greeted me. They were all excited to meet me, and a few guys in particular were eager to show me their work. We walked out into an open field, and I saw my tarp. They had welded together pieces of metal so that the tarp hung perfectly in place. It was just like the one at home. Relief washed over me as I became confident that at least I could keep up my practice routine.

As the week got going, it was incredible to see Ellen in her element. For the first time, I got to see parts of her heart that I had only heard about. Watching Ellen love the people of Zambia taught me a lot about passion. When you are passionate about something, you give it everything you've got. Passion gets down so deep inside of you that you feel like, if you don't do something about it, your heart might explode. I knew Ellen was passionate about Africa. But watching her pick up one child after another, hugging them all like they were her own, allowed me to see how God uniquely fits passion with a heart.

I could identify with how Ellen felt. I saw her come alive as she engaged the Zambian orphans, and I realized that the pitching mound is where I come alive. God's goodness is so real to me when I'm playing the game I love. So I know what it's like to feel passionate. For years, Ellen had supported me in my passion. She flew all over the country, staying in sketchy hotels near my place or on an air mattress with other girlfriends, to watch me play. Now it was my turn to come into her world.

At the end of our first day of manual labor in Zambia, we were all wiped out. We had spent the majority of the afternoon mixing cement, a project that takes its toll on your entire body. When we got back to the complex where we were staying, I rallied to go throw the baseball before the sun went down. A few of the guys on the trip had played baseball in high school, and they had brought their gloves with them to play some catch. Right outside of the complex stretched a long dirt road. I stood on one side and started doing some long toss across the road to another guy. Nearby, I could hear children still laughing and playing at the end of the day. We were staying close to a village. As we threw back and forth, I noticed a few kids wander over to get a closer look. They seemed intrigued by what we were doing. Heads bobbed up and down over the tall grass as kids ran through the field that separated our hotel from their village. Soon enough, the dirt street was lined with African children watching the ball go back and forth. With each throw, they cheered a little louder. For many, this was the first time they had seen an American baseball. The cheers got louder and louder, and soon I couldn't help but laugh. I looked over at a young boy standing right next to me. I motioned to him to hold out his hands, and then I gently tossed him the ball. He broke into a hysterical laugh, and soon the whole crowd of children laughed with him. I held up my glove as he tossed the ball back. The children crowded around, forming a line to be the next one to catch a ball. The other guys with gloves caught on, and soon clumps of kids scurried around to join various lines.

As the sun set over the dirt road, we played catch with a crowd of Zambian orphans. I handed off my glove and, one kid at a time, taught them how to wear it and how to use it. The excitement on their faces reminded me of how much I love baseball. I feel like that every time I play. It was amazing to teach these kids about something that is as natural as breathing for me. Watching them figure out baseball was awesome. I felt like I was learning to love them in my own language. Suddenly it clicked. I realized how I could use the gifts the Lord had given me to relate to these kids. The Lord provided an avenue for me to show them a new world and my passion—baseball. My glove swallowed each tiny hand, but they quickly figured out how to compensate. I tossed the ball to them underhand, and then they would send it flying back overhand—just as we had been doing earlier. I was amazed by their perception. They copied us perfectly. We played until the sun sank below the horizon and the kids slowly trickled back toward the community.

That day, on a dirt road in Africa, something amazing happened: I saw two passions collide. Standing in the middle of Africa—Ellen's passion—I taught children to play baseball—my passion. For years, I had thought our different passions were too far apart to ever intersect. I never imagined a moment like the one that took place during that January sunset. For the first time, our two passions stood side by side. It's a powerful thing when passions collide. The Lord started something that day that Ellen and I will spend a lifetime exploring.

We are learning new ways to join in the Lord's work in Africa, including through baseball. Partnering with a ministry called Arise Africa, we started "Kershaw's Challenge," a program to help raise support for the orphans of Zambia. It's our way of combining baseball and mission work. For every strikeout I made during the season, we gave a donation toward work in Zambia. Arise Africa has opened an awesome opportunity for us. Our goal is one day to build an orphanage to be a home and refuge for children. Lord willing, this new orphanage will be called "Hope's Home"—in honor of our friend Hope. We want to give Hope and children with similar stories a place to finally call home. It's a lofty goal, but we have been encouraged by the awesome ways the Lord has already provided. Many people have joined in our efforts—including several Little League and high school pitchers from Texas, who are making donations with each of their own strikeouts as well. It's been overwhelming to see the support and growing awareness for the needs in Africa. Ellen and I share big dreams for that continent, and we can't wait to see how the Lord will use our two passions to do great things for His glory.

I left the old blue pitching tarp in Zambia, as my way of saying that I'll be back. We plan on continuing to participate in the work that the Lord has started. There is always more to do. In particular, I'll return to that dirt road. I'll stand with a couple of gloves and hope that my friends from the villages come back to play catch. This is just the beginning. Passions can take you to some pretty incredible places. I never imagined that baseball would take me to a long dirt road in the middle of Africa.

# Epilogue

Ann Higginbottom

**On December 4, 2010, I found myself standing at the front of a church with Clayton.** It was the same church where I grew up and got married. Clayton and I were both waiting anxiously for the big moment. The doors at the back of the sanctuary would open and my sister—his bride—would come walking toward us.

As the doors opened, Ellen was confident and radiant. All eyes were on her, except for the occasional glance to see Clayton's response. I'll never forget the way Ellen looked that day. It was such a privilege to stand beside her as she married the man I already loved like a little brother. Over the years, Clayton had become such a natural part of our family. Making it "official" made perfect sense to me. Clayton and Ellen are perfect for each other, and I knew that day was the beginning of something extraordinary.

In the summer of 2009, I traveled to Africa with Ellen. Determined to see what had so quickly captured her heart, my little brother, John, and I hopped on the long flight to Lusaka with our sister. Ellen was our enthusiastic guide, and we got to see some incredible sights. The moment the Zambian kids saw Ellen, they swarmed her. Jumping, hugging and singing, they wouldn't let her go. The more I saw, the more I finally understood the deepest part of my sister's heart. Her heart broke, bled and rejoiced for Africa.

That summer, I gained a new understanding of Ellen. And for the first time, I was able to see the redemptive work the Lord is doing in Zambia. I had this undeniable feeling that we were on the front edge of something great. I saw Africa because my sister taught me how to see.

I had the chance to visit Ellen and Clayton as they spent their first year of marriage together in Los Angeles. Something about their new life caught my attention. In the midst of Major League Baseball and the glitz of Los Angeles, they were delightfully the same funny pair they were back home. Nothing had changed. They seemed to enjoy the beauty of insignificance—slipping into the background and living simply.

When I drove to Dodger Stadium with them, I had a rare glimpse into their lives. With the windows rolled down, they stopped at every security point and parking lot to greet the stadium crew by name. Ellen and Clayton asked people personal questions about their families and drove away with the promise to see them again the next day. People matter to this couple. It was refreshing to watch two young people who were marching to a different beat. In the stir of Los Angeles chaos, they were content to lead quiet, intentional lives.

One early morning in July, Clayton called with some news. He quickly apologized for the late notice but informed me that he wouldn't be able to come home during the All-Star break as in years before. I paused in confusion. He then proceeded to share the news that he had been selected to the 2011 National League All-Star team. It was another dream come true, and our family rejoiced with Ellen and Clayton. In mid-July, the Kershaws traveled to Phoenix, Arizona, for the eighty-second exhibition game. The entire experience was humbling and exciting for them. Back home in Texas, we kept our fingers crossed that Clayton would get to come into the game. In the fifth inning, he came trotting from the dugout and took the mound. Eight pitches later, he had retired the American League side. The moment was brief, but the memories of his first All-Star game will last a lifetime.

My sister and Clayton never went looking for attention. They have simply planted their feet right where the Lord has called them to be. When the thought of a book surfaced, they were hesitant. They quickly said, "We don't have much of a story to tell, and we really don't want it to be all about us."

I encouraged them to think about it in a different light. "What if the Lord wants to write a story through you? What if a book could highlight the Lord's faithfulness and His work in Africa? What if writing a book could encourage a younger generation to know and rely on the Lord's love?" They liked that idea. But they didn't want the attention, only the privilege of doing something to make the Lord look great.

As Clayton committed his season to the Lord, big things started to happen. He would never tell you about the accolades that came his way after the 2011 baseball season—if you ask him about the year, I'm sure he would give the glory to the Lord and the credit to his teammates—but as the Dodgers' season came to a close, Clayton had achieved the rare "Triple Crown" as a pitcher. He led the National League in strikeouts (248), wins (21) and earned run average (2.28). Yet while he was setting new career highs in these categories, he never talked about the statistics. He simply worked hard and enjoyed playing the game he loved. He knew the Lord had given him the ability to play, and he was grateful that he could help others as he did what he loved. I tease Clayton endlessly about his humility, but I can't think of a more God-glorifying way to live a life.

Ellen and Clayton went home to Dallas after the season, but the good news kept coming. Clayton received the Warren Spahn Award, given by the Oklahoma Sports Museum for the best left-handed pitcher in baseball. Additionally, and much to his surprise, Clayton received a Gold Glove from Rawlings for his defensive performance as a pitcher. Whenever Clayton pitched, he seemed to find opportunities to run, slide and dive to make plays and get outs. Occasionally a batter would hit a line drive right at him. My family would wince as Clayton did everything he could to catch it. The combination of being really competitive and feeling fairly invincible makes for some exciting defensive moments. I suppose all of the acrobatic plays caught the attention of the voters who gave him this honor.

Since 1956, Major League Baseball has presented the Cy Young Award to the best pitchers in baseball. The Cy Young—which is given to one pitcher in the American League and one in the National League—is the highest honor a pitcher can receive. Throughout the season, we heard speculation that Clayton might be in the running for the award, and the rumors increased late in the season. When we asked Clayton about it, he would quickly brush it off and remind us that there were so many guys who deserved it more than him. Then in November 2011 the votes came in. Clayton won the Cy Young Award for the National League. Although many would argue that he deserved such an honor, he would rather give the honor to the Lord.

While it is an honor to be recognized by the League, a nod of approval by Clayton's fellow teammates means even more to him. After the 2011 season, Clayton was named the National League Outstanding Pitcher by the Player's Choice Awards. These individual awards are voted on by the players themselves, and this acknowledgement was a tremendous encouragement to Clayton.

More than the awards, Ellen and Clayton have been amazed at how the Lord has blessed Kershaw's Challenge. Through the generosity of many people, the Kershaws have raised enough money to break ground on Hope's Home in Lusaka, Zambia. Ellen's passion, now shared with Clayton, will reach new levels. Today they continue to raise support and awareness for the desperate needs of Africa. Although the needs are overwhelming, the Kershaws speak with a voice of hope. They have seen what the Lord has already done, so they have great confidence that He will continue to do great things in Zambia and across the continent. Ellen and Clayton can envision a bright future for the children of Africa.

In January, I have the privilege of accompanying Clayton and Ellen as they return to Africa. I will meet Hope and see the beginning of a dream: an orphanage built as a refuge for the children my sister taught me to love. Our prayer is that others would begin to think and move toward Africa, or whatever mission field the Lord may have for them, at home or abroad.

The beauty of a story involving two young people is that, Lord willing, this is only the beginning. Ellen and Clayton share a unique heart. Their passions began to grow in the early years of their childhood, and at the right time, the Lord brought them together. They make each other better. They help each other live for the Lord. Years after they met as kids, they find themselves in a remarkable place—finding joy in people and baseball, with hearts that beat for the children of Africa.

# Acknowledgments

We never intended to share this story—especially in the form of a book. The Lord surprised us with the opportunity and taught us a lot along the way. As we began to write, we realized that this isn't just our story. The Lord has brought people into our lives at the perfect time to make a lasting impression. This book is the tale of all those who have come alongside us and shared life with us. A simple "thank you" doesn't even seem adequate. We're humbled to see how our story is covered with the grace of God, rooted in the love of our families, and filled with good friendships. This is not just our story—this is your story, too.

To Ann—we wouldn't have wanted to share the journey of writing this book with anyone else. You helped us find the Lord's work in our lives. Your writing gift has touched the lives of many, and it will continue to be used to glorify the One who gave it to you. Thank you for walking with us as a mentor, encourager, counselor and partner throughout the process.

To our friends—many of you remember every detail of our story, even the awkward years. You grew up with us and made every step of the way memorable. Thank you for dreaming with us and for being faithful reminders that the Lord has blessed our path immensely. Here's to the years to come! And a special note of gratitude to the Los Angeles Dodgers for your support along the way, and the chance to live out a dream.

To our families—you are the backbone of our story. Your love for us is written into the fabric of this book. We hope that you can laugh at the memories and be encouraged by the Lord's hand at work. When our dreams seemed impossible and the leap of faith too scary, your words of affirmation kept us going. We have big dreams. You help us believe that they are possible. Sharing life with you is one of the greatest blessings of our lives.

# About the Writer

Ann Higginbottom grew up in Dallas, Texas, with her parents, her sister, Ellen, and two brothers. As Ellen's sister and Clayton's sister-in-law, Ann has a unique angle to help the Kershaws tell their story. Ann has witnessed every stage of Clayton and Ellen's relationship, so she was thrilled to have the opportunity to work with them on this book.

Ann loves watching Dodger baseball, her puppy Maverick, and anything that has to do with the beach. In 2007 she published *The Work of the Lord: Seaside Reflections*. Her first book includes devotionals and photography rooted in Amelia Island, Florida, where Ann spent summers with her family growing up. (For more information, visit www.workoftheLord.com.) Since then, she has worked on various other books of her own and partnered with other authors.

Ann has been married to Robby for three years. They live in Dallas, where Ann continues to pursue her passion for writing and photography. Ann and Robby enjoy spending time with their family and friends and serving the Lord at Park Cities Presbyterian Church.

Clayton and Ellen at the Gold Glove Award banquet in New York City.

# CONGRATULATIONS TO CLAYTON KERSHAW

## 2011 Honors and Accomplishments:

National League Cy Young Award Winner
National League Pitchers Triple Crown Winner
Warren Spahn Award (best left-handed pitcher)
Rawlings Gold Glove Award Winner (for defense)
Players Choice Award for Outstanding Pitcher in the National League
*Sporting News* National League Pitcher of the Year
National League All-Star Team Selection

This is a tremendous honor, perfectly fitting someone who this season became one of the best pitchers in Major League Baseball. We have witnessed a young person learn, compete and develop a rare talent leading to his winning of baseball's most prestigious pitching award.

### NED COLLETTI
Dodger General Manager

I am first and foremost a big fan of Clayton and have been honored to watch his quest in moving from good to great. He's just scratching the surface of what he can become, and I know he can reach much higher limits. Congratulations, Clayton, it's an amazing honor.

### OREL HERSHISER
1988 NL Cy Young Award Winner and World Champion Los Angeles Dodgers Pitcher

I'm extremely happy for Clayton and his family. He definitely deserved the Cy Young, and being just the sixteenth pitcher to be the triple crown winner makes it even more special. Clayton has always separated himself at every level with his hard work, preparation, and determination to be the best he can be. He is a model for all of our pitchers in our organization to follow. I hope this is the first of many Cy Young awards for him.

### RICK HONEYCUTT
Dodger Pitching Coach

Clayton Kershaw is very deserving of this award. He is one of the fiercest competitors I have seen and plays the game the way it is supposed to be played. He has improved each year, and last season he did it all. Congratulations, as it is well deserved.

## TOMMY LASORDA
Dodger Special Advisor to the Chairman

Clayton represents everything good about this game and this award. He is a tremendous worker, a student of baseball and a great teammate. He's always trying to get better and deserves all the accolades that come his way.

## DON MATTINGLY
Dodger Manager

As the winner of the first Cy Young Award, I am so very proud of Clayton Kershaw and his outstanding performances that led to his receiving the 2011 Cy Young Award. I am reminded of Sandy Koufax whenever I see Clayton pitch and feel that there is a deep comparison between the two. Clayton has an outstanding work ethic, as did Sandy, which will show itself through Clayton's baseball career.

## DON NEWCOMBE
Dodger Special Advisor to the Chairman
1956 Dodger Cy Young Award Winner

The only thing winning the Cy Young does for Clayton is that he'll expect more of himself in 2012. He's a very special young man!

## JOE TORRE
Former Dodger Manager

## Clayton's Stats

|  | ERA | W | L | SO | WHIP |
|---|---|---|---|---|---|
| 2011 Regular Season | 2.28 | 21 | 5 | 248 | 0.98 |
| Career | 2.88 | 47 | 28 | 745 | 1.17 |

# KERSHAW'S CHALLENGE

★ ★ ★ ★ ★ ★ ★ ★ ★ ★ ★

*Strikeout to Serve*

Kershaw's Challenge is a result of two passions: baseball and Africa. In January 2011, Clayton and Ellen Kershaw, as newlyweds, traveled to Africa together for the first time to continue a work that Ellen had begun years before. During that trip, Clayton was introduced to the country, people and joyful children that had changed Ellen's perspective.

When they returned home to Texas, Kershaw's Challenge was born. Clayton and Ellen decided to donate $100 for every batter he struck out during the 2011 baseball season. The money went directly toward making life better for children in Zambia. Their dream was to create a safe haven and welcoming home for orphans and children in desperate situations. Lord willing, this home will become a reality in 2012.

With each new baseball season, Kershaw's Challenge will continue—aiming at a new goal each year. As the Lord leads, Clayton and Ellen are determined to glorify God through the physical and spiritual nurture of children in need. And they welcome you to join them in the challenge as new opportunities arise.

## WWW.KERSHAWSCHALLENGE.COM